Black Sheep and Prodigals

An antidote to black and white religion

Dave Tomlinson

With illustrations by Rob Pepper

HODDER

First published in Great Britain in 2017 by Hodder & Stoughton
An Hachette UK company

This paperback edition with additional chapter first published in 2018

1

A CIP catalogue record for this title is available from the British Library

ISBN 978 1 473 61104 7
eBook ISBN 978 1 473 61103 0

Typeset in Sabon MT by Hewer Text UK Ltd, Edinburgh
Printed and bound in the UK by CPI Group (UK) Ltd, Croydon CR0 4YY

Hodder & Stoughton policy is to use papers that are natural, renewable
and recyclable products and made from wood grown in sustainable
forests. The logging and manufacturing processes are expected to
conform to the environmental regulations of the country of origin.

Hodder & Stoughton Ltd
Carmelite House
50 Victoria Embankment
London EC4Y 0DZ

www.hodderfaith.com

To the Revd Peter Thomson, my dearly departed friend and black sheep mentor. The most generously minded man I ever met.

Contents

Prelude: Not for the spiritually certain

For my part I know nothing with any certainty,
but the sight of stars makes me dream.

Vincent van Gogh

I am a black sheep. I suspect I may have a conformity defi-cit. As soon as someone utters a certainty, or tells me that I have to *do* this or *believe* that, the opposite comes to mind. My dad preferred to call it being pig-headed – to which I would (pig-headedly) reply, 'Well, it takes one to know one!'

I definitely don't wish to promote stubbornness to the status of a virtue, and I regret my youthful obstinacy with my dad, but I do think it's important in life to discover what *you* believe instead of being pressured into going along with the crowd. Authenticity is a basic spiritual quality.

Religion, on the other hand, often seems to require conformity. The Church has a long history of suppress-ing dissenting voices – with heresy trials, grand inquisi-tions and witch-hunts. It's an approach that has mostly disappeared now, but faith is still something that folk can be very black and white about. At one extreme some people will blow up planes, shoot holidaymakers or drive trucks into crowds of shoppers because they believe that they are serving the purpose of God. But even at a much more innocent level, there are plenty of people who are so certain their version of religion is correct that they will write off everyone who disagrees.

This book isn't for the spiritually certain. It's for people who are fed up with black and white religion, who long for something more humane and open ended. It's for the multitudes who may be on the edges or outside of mainstream religion, who reject traditional interpretations of Christianity yet would like to believe.

A short while back, I gave a talk to an audience of predominantly churchgoing people, many of whom didn't appear to like my approach to faith. After a period of antagonistic questioning, a young man asked if he could say something. 'I'm not a churchgoer,' he confessed; 'I'm an atheist. Actually, I'm only here because my girlfriend brought me. I have been to lots of church events with her, and mostly, it all sounds like gobbledegook. But what I have heard tonight almost persuades me to believe in God – not just because of what the speaker said, but because of the way he said it. It felt like I was being invited into an adult conversation about God – one in which my views would genuinely be taken into account – instead of just listening to a monologue.'

I can see why some people find black and white certainty attractive: it means never having to rethink things, never being confronted by a reality that you can't understand, never having to really engage with things which are unfamiliar or foreign – always feeling safe in the security of the sheepfold. But this is cloud cuckoo land, not reality. As Benjamin Franklin said, only two things in life are certain: death and taxes.

I know that St Paul had a 'Damascus Road experience' (he invented the idea actually) when he saw a great light and was converted, but I confess I am mostly quite wary of people who see great lights. I am more inclined towards the experience of the former Poet Laureate, Andrew Motion, who said, 'I've seen the light. And it flickers on and off like a badly wired lamp.' He goes on to say that this is probably the experience of millions of people who inhabit what he calls the 'ambivalent middle ground in religion'.

This book is of the 'badly wired lamp' variety – directed at those millions on the ambivalent middle ground. I am not trying to say, 'Here is the truth. I've found it!' I am a wandering black sheep looking down some intriguing back lanes trying to discover a faith I really can believe in. I hope you'll join me.

1. I believe in being true to yourself

find your inner black sheep

To go wrong in one's own way is better than to go right in someone else's.

Fyodor Dostoyevsky

Having barely darkened a church doorway for twenty years, Nina never imagined joining one – much less loving it. She still shuns the label 'Christian', admits to struggling with the version of God she finds in the Bible, and most of the time can't stand Jesus – at least, not the Jesus she has often heard talked about in church. Yet she has found a home in our church community.

She tried being a Christian when she was younger, even got confirmed (or was it 'conformed'?) at thirteen. But in the end she was turned off by the judgementalism she detected in the Church: 'This obsession with personal morality. Everyone convinced of their rightness and everyone else's wrongness.'

By her late teens Nina was exploring Buddhism and stopped calling herself a Christian. Friends at university persuaded her to accompany them to church a couple of times, but her heart wasn't in it. And it would just wind her up.

Now a single mum, Nina says a big part of the explanation for being part of a church lies with Isaac, her son. She always wanted him raised in a community with strong values, 'where people asked questions about right and wrong, about the purpose of life – where you could think about bigger things than the latest Nike trainers or TV show'.

Before finding St Luke's she went on a bit of a quest, visiting the Unitarians, the Quakers, the Buddhists, but despite feeling at home with some of them, they weren't really set up for children. Then Jonathan and Denise, a couple she met when she was pregnant, and members of

St Luke's, invited her to join them. She wondered what the church would think of her coming – even though she didn't believe in God or the Bible, and didn't like Jesus. Jonathan said it was fine; they'd take anyone.

As a penance for her 'bad thoughts about Jesus', Nina signed up to the coffee rota. And now, ten years on, she's the 'unofficial Director of After-Church Beverages'!

'It's the community I was looking for,' she says: 'relaxed, open, accepting. I even find the talks inspiring. It's a place where I try to embody my own spiritual practice, which is Buddhist.'

If she had a creed, Nina says the key words would be 'kindness' and 'forgiveness', 'compassion', 'courage' and 'patience'; with 'community' and 'family' also near the top.

But words like this are useless in isolation, she stresses: 'You have to embody your faith. There's nothing wrong with sitting in a cave meditating, but you only find out what it means when you leave the cave behind. When you engage with the real world.'

The Buddhist emphasis on practice rather than belief really makes sense to Nina. 'It underlines how every day we try to walk the talk,' she says. 'We don't always get it right, but we reflect and we go again. Our practice includes our mistakes. We're never qualified, we're always practising.'

And after ten years at St Luke's, Nina has even come to think differently about Jesus. Although she sees two Jesuses. 'The one you often find talked about in church – judgemental, separating people, focused on the good and the bad' – she still finds that Jesus hard to take. But then there's another Jesus for whom she has a lot of time – who she says was 'probably a Buddhist. Like me.'*

Nina isn't the average church member. She practises Buddhism, questions the Bible and holds less than conventional thoughts about God and Jesus. On which basis, many churches definitely wouldn't accept her as a member. At the very least she would be perceived as spiritually prodigal, a wandering black sheep needing to find the fold of true faith. Maybe she would be invited onto an Alpha course or the like to get 'converted', to discover the true way.

Nina *is* a black sheep, I agree. But in a good sense. She is her own person, not just one of the crowd. Her spirituality arises from experience. There is nothing prepackaged about her. She has her own values, beliefs and practices that she has thought about and internalised. She is a woman of considerable spiritual intelligence.

---

* Nina's story appears in full in Martin Wroe, *The Gospel According to Everyone* (lulu.com, 2011).

Actually, we all have an inner black sheep, a wayward independent side, and our spiritual development depends on finding it and learning to integrate it into our daily lives. It's the instinct to question the status quo, to swim against the tide, to explore a different path, to be authentic. Our more controlling, fearful self tells us not to listen to our questioning self; to step back in line, keep the rules and fit in, play things safe. But until we begin to accept and engage this spiritual shadow side to us we cannot really grow in faith, or even as individuals.

The Quaker Parker Palmer writes, 'I want to learn how to hold the paradoxical poles of my identity together, to embrace the profoundly opposite truths that my sense of self is deeply dependent on others dancing with me and that I still have a sense of self when no one wants to dance.'* Black sheep spirituality focuses on this tension. It is not about being a loner or spurning community, but about learning to value our own instincts at least as much as we do those of others, and having the courage to stand by them.

The natural assumption is that churches and other religious groups will be obvious settings to grow our spiritual intelligence. And sometimes they are. However, emails

---

* Parker J. Palmer, *The Courage to Teach: Exploring the Inner Landscape of a Teacher's Life* (Jossey Bass, 2007).

and messages I receive most days of my life say something different. Even as I write, a woman from New Zealand tells me that she feels her church is more of a religious kindergarten than the 'university of the spirit' that she hoped for. 'There is no room for me to live, breathe, be my own person,' she writes. 'If I am going to be accepted, I'll need to fit in, to be a virtual carbon copy of everyone else. But I won't be that.'

The Church haemorrhages people like this all the time. They are the black sheep, the prodigals prone to wandering from the well-worn path, who ask the 'wrong' questions, struggle to fit in. Yet often they are the ones who are the most perceptive and spiritually switched on. Conformity is *not* a fruit of the Spirit. Quite the reverse: it is a product of fear and intimidation.

For twenty-five years, these kinds of people have been the main focus of my life and work – people on the edges of the religious ghetto, or completely outside of it, yet whose spiritual journeys are often more authentic than those of many insiders.

This very week, in a pub after a wedding I conducted, I had umpteen conversations with people of considerable spiritual nous who had long ago stopped going to church because they were frustrated by the unquestioning conformity they felt was required of them. 'Of course, that's not how people in the Church would see it,' one man told me. 'They'd say that they welcome you asking questions. But once you make it clear that you aren't going to tow the line, that you hold a different point of view about God or Jesus or something, you're looked at with suspicion. You're not a kosher Christian unless you believe the "right" things.'

Another man spoke with some concern about his two grown-up children who no longer went to church or believed the same things as him and his wife. 'But look at them,' I replied. 'They are fine human beings, clearly driven by spiritual values, even if they no longer find church and conventional faith attractive or helpful. If I were you, I'd be proud of them.'

'You're right,' he said. 'The truth is, they've had the courage to ask the questions I have always pushed to the back of my mind. We're not so different really; it's just the way we've handled our doubts.'

For ten years in the 1990s, I led a 'church' in a pub, known self-disparagingly as 'Holy Joes', especially designed for church prodigals. Nowadays I am the vicar of a more conventional-looking church, yet which is virtually a flock of black sheep: people who want to have their own opinions, who dislike being told what to believe and often question things; who want to be authentic. These are my people. This is where I feel at home: at the edges of faith.

Christian spirituality is too often understood and couched in passive terms like 'obedience' and 'submission', as if we were meant to be compliant infants instead of grown adults with questions and healthy scepticism and a voice to speak back. So we end up with a religious subculture of conformity, where fear inhibits any sense of real faith and adventure.

In many churches, especially those of the more conservative ilk, the culture of conformity is intentionally nurtured in the name of 'holiness' or 'discipleship'. God may be perceived as a father, but definitely an authority figure with a plan for people's lives that must be known and obeyed. So being a 'good' Christian involves becoming weak and dependent in some way – certainly dependent on the Almighty, but maybe also on the church leaders as God's representatives. And phrases like 'only believe', 'trust and obey' and 'lean not on your own understanding' become mantras that cultivate a mentality of learned helplessness, a psychology of compliance.

Ron grew up in this kind of church culture, and up until his mid-twenties looked like the perfect model of a 'good' Christian. He 'gave his heart to Jesus' when he was thirteen, was baptised as an adult two years later, and by the time he was nineteen was helping to lead an Alpha group in the church, with no awareness of any serious questions or queries about his faith. 'I was like a perfect sheep,' he told me, 'heading in the same direction as everyone else, never questioning whether it was the right direction, never doubting what I was told, never allowing myself any stray thoughts.'

Then life at university brought Ron a raft of doubts and questions. Perhaps it was living away from home and not going to his church regularly, or maybe issues raised by his coursework, or just beginning to see Christianity through the eyes of his non-churchgoing friends, but his faith began to unravel. 'It was as if I was suddenly outside the bubble of certainty and unquestioning compliance,' he said. 'It was kind of scary, but also liberating.'

By complete contrast with the approach Ron experienced in his church background, Tom, the head of RE in a comprehensive school in Essex, told me that his real objective in teaching religion, ethics and philosophy is to help students to think for themselves, to find an opinion. A lot of the young people in his school come from unreflective secular homes and backgrounds, where religion and faith are hardly even mentioned. But it doesn't much matter whether we are model religious sheep or model secular sheep, a sheep (in these terms) is a sheep: someone trapped in a 'sheepfold' of unquestioned assumptions, meekly heading in the same direction, maybe very bright or intellectual, yet spiritually unawakened, seldom applying themselves to the big questions.

Knowing that there are people like Tom teaching our young people gives me great hope, but there are too few of them. Education should not be about creating good hoop-jumpers who can navigate their way through the predictable demands of the system, or spew out memorised information for an exam; it should be about enabling students to think for themselves, to become curious, to engage with life imaginatively and discover their own mind, to establish their own values and measures of success.

Similarly, church should not be a place to absorb hand-me-down information about God and Christianity, or to become conformed to a given Christian outlook. I believe we need church communities that are 'laboratories of the Spirit' – places where we can explore issues of faith and spirituality with openness, imagination and creativity. In an era when fundamentalist certainty on the one hand and wishy-washy moralism on the other, appear to many outside the Church to be the only options on offer, we need hotbeds of passionate diversity, schools of independent thinking and believing, spirited settings of debate and difference where multiple integrities can co-exist in friendship and love.

Such communities will nurture what I'm calling black sheep spirituality, an approach to faith:

- that can embrace a particular tradition (in my case Christianity) without assuming that it has an exclusive claim to truth;
- that sits comfortably with doubts and questions as an essential part of faith;
- that recognises dissent and difference of opinion as something to cultivate, as a sign of a secure community;
- that affirms the necessity of constantly renewing, reinterpreting and reforming beliefs in the light of new insights, new challenges, new situations;
- that embraces divine revelation wherever it may be found – in art and science and the natural world as well as in religious traditions; in the universal human experience of friendship, compassion and justice;
- that treats faith as something to be lived and practised, not embalmed in rational beliefs or religious rituals.

11

Black sheep spirituality is not a new thing. The Church has always produced its prodigals: people who have swum against the tide, thought outside the box or disobeyed the rules in their pursuit of greater understanding. Sometimes they have been left out, or labelled 'heretic', or suffered exclusion – or worse.

Isn't it interesting that the term 'heresy' originally referred to the 'act of choosing'? To be a heretic simply meant to 'choose for oneself'. But over time it came to indicate a belief or an opinion deemed unacceptable, an idea or interpretation that deviated from the recognised position of the Church or the establishment. Yet surely it is a good thing for people to think for themselves, even if the rest of us disagree with their conclusions. Surely it is the sign of a strong group or society when it allows for dissent – and, indeed, fights for the right of a person to disagree.

James, in the New Testament, argues vigorously that faith isn't primarily about words but actions. We can argue till the cows come home about words and beliefs, but it is how we live that demonstrates the sincerity and legitimacy of our faith.

The real heresy in our world is the evil that people do to one another and to the planet – especially in God's name or in the service of God. Killing and abusing, persecuting minorities or people of difference, creating and sustaining systems of economic and social injustice, destroying the environment and our fellow creatures on Earth – these are the genuine heresies. Not views and beliefs that happen to depart from a prevailing Church consensus.

It's easy to forget that the teaching and practice of Jesus was considered heresy by some of the Jewish leaders of his time – for which they colluded with the Romans to have him killed. He was a black sheep, a loose cannon: a prodigal who wandered outside their idea of what was true or acceptable. Yet in reality his crucifixion had much more to do with the threat he posed to their corrupt leadership – the threat that is always posed to established authorities by those who stand apart from the crowd, who take a different position, who refuse simply to conform, or who question the prevailing 'wisdom'.

In a way we must all be heretics in this sense: people who make responsible choices about what to believe and how to live. More importantly, we need those communities strong enough to hold us together in our difference, where common values of love and friendship and justice are more important than doctrinal conformity.

This book is an exercise in black sheep spirituality. It is my attempt to give an honest snapshot of what my faith means – and what it doesn't mean – without needing to justify it with proof texts from the Bible or making reference to existing ideas and interpretations. It isn't a blueprint for other black sheep or 'bad Christians'; it's more of a summary of my own faith-in-progress – and a provocation for you to go on a similar journey.

2. I believe beliefs are overrated

they are only words after all

*I am very cautious of people who are absolutely
right, especially when they are vehemently so.*

Michael Palin

When I told a neighbour who says she doesn't believe in
God that fifteen Muslim students came to our Midnight
Mass at Christmas, *and* they received Communion, she
literally wept for joy in the street.

'Go steady, Dave,' she told me. 'You're going to get

me out of bed on a Sunday morning if you're not careful!'

Most of us have had enough of black and white religion – not just when it leads to suicide bombings and terrorist attacks, but also when people insist on having a monopoly on God, or truth about God.

To be honest, I had no idea that the group of students were Muslims. Midnight Mass is always bursting with visitors, and faces I don't recognise. The students were just part of the crowd, with no particular indication that they were of a different faith.

When midnight struck, the church descended into customary delightful chaos with everyone wishing those around them a happy Christmas, and sharing the peace of Christ with a handshake or a hug.

A few minutes later, we stood around the altar (we have a large round altar table in the centre of the church) to celebrate the first mass of Christmas. This is the point at which, in many churches, an invisible line divides the 'innies' from the 'outies' – those who qualify to receive Communion from those who don't. No such distinction exists at St Luke's. Our approach to Communion is based on the example of Jesus in the Gospels where he ate and drank with all and sundry – often including people who were snubbed or rejected by the religious establishment, so-called 'sinners'.

I therefore offered the invitation I give every Sunday:

> This is the table of Jesus Christ where all are welcome and no one is turned away. We therefore offer bread and wine to every single person here, without exception. If you would like to receive Communion, please come forward now. God welcomes all.

As people came forward for Communion, it was clear that more than usual opted for the non-alcoholic alternative to wine, but it never occurred to me that this was because some were Muslims.

Afterwards, the students beamed as they spoke of the warm welcome they found among us. 'With all the hatred and violence going on in the world, we wanted to join with Christian brothers and sisters in celebrating the birth of Jesus,' one young man told me with a broad grin and a twinkly eye. It was their first experience of being in a church. And neither they nor we will forget it.

The following day, in a Christmas post on Facebook, I told the story of our midnight encounter with visitors 'from the East', maintaining that a common humanity is surely more important than religious denomination.

Many people 'liked' the post, but there were also comments and emails from people who disagreed. Some made reference to St Paul's warning about eating the bread and drinking the wine 'unworthily'. I replied that Paul's comments had nothing to do with whether people believed the 'right' things or belonged to the 'correct' religious group. It was about people behaving in the wrong way. It was about division and discrimination in the community, about people showing contempt instead of compassion. Ultimately it was about not recognising God in the other.*

One email I received stated emphatically that the God Muslims worship is not the same God that Christians worship. But how could anyone know this? Yes, we have different doctrines and beliefs about God that can't simply be set aside, but as we shall discuss later in the book, this may simply express the impossibility of any human words or categories to define or contain God.

Surely it is time to stop stating categorically what we cannot possibly know for certain. In a world torn apart by black and white religious assertions about God and the will of God, surely we need the humility to stick with what we can be sure of: that love always trumps beliefs.

---

* 1 Corinthians 11:17–22.

And actually, the presence of the Muslims at Midnight Mass seems wonderfully appropriate. After all, according to Matthew's Gospel, the infant Jesus was visited by well-wishers from the East: the Magi or 'Wise Men', Persian astrologers, probably Zoroastrians. There is no suggestion in this interfaith event that the visitors converted to Judaism, much less Christianity. To them, Jesus did not appear as a sectarian figure, but the bearer of good news to all people. And I'm sure they never left without sharing a meal or two with the holy family and others – a *de facto* act of Communion to celebrate the birth of the child.

I did not set out to offer Communion to a group of young Muslims at Midnight Mass, but I am extremely glad I did. To have refused them would surely be the equivalent of sending the Magi packing with gifts unopened.

In my younger days, I looked for God in 'Christian' activities: Bible reading, prayers, church worship and the like – all of which still have their place in my life, though the nature of them has radically changed with the years. But now I see that my whole faith existed at the time within a tiny religious bubble, when in fact the whole Earth was full of God's glory. My God was far too small.

There is a lovely story about two learned men walking along the seashore, engaged in vigorous debate about the nature of God and the meaning of life. As they strolled along they came upon a small boy playing on the beach. He had dug a hole in the sand and kept running to the sea to fetch water in his bucket, which he then poured into the hole. It was a never-ending task.

The two men watched the boy with amusement as he sped to and fro filling and emptying his bucket. One of them teasingly asked the boy what he was doing. Almost too busy to speak, the boy earnestly replied that he was emptying the sea into the hole. The men smiled and walked on, resuming their argument. Then one of them stopped, looked back at the boy, and said, 'You know, we're trying to do what this little boy is doing. It's just as impossible to understand the mystery of God as it is for the boy to put the sea into the hole in the sand. Our minds are just tiny thimbles, while the reality of God is as vast as the ocean.'

It's only a story, but I hope the men continued their discussion, debating long and hard as they walked along the beach. There are no final answers. No ultimate conclusions. Yet the need to probe and search and imagine is embedded in the human psyche. It is what faith is about, what life is about. Not settled certainties or neatly packed solutions, but a passionate quest, a journey of exploration, where doubt and scepticism are as important as belief and conviction.

Like the men in the story, I too enjoy chewing on the big issues, arguing and reasoning about God, life and the meaning of everything. I love to. I need to. Yet when all is said and done, I know I am but a small boy digging holes in the sand, and when the tide comes in, my little excavations – my stuttering efforts at truth – will be swamped and swallowed up by a boundless ocean too vast to comprehend. Faith, finally, is not about words. It is not about concepts and beliefs, no matter how profound. Faith is entrusting one's self to the eternal mystery which cannot be reduced to human ideas and categories.

Not everyone agrees, I know. People with a more black and white approach will say that faith necessarily means believing certain things. That the Bible is the Word of God, say. Or that Mary was a virgin. Or that Jesus physically rose from the dead and ascended into heaven on a cloud. Or that other religions are wrong. The list may vary, but the insistence remains the same: we *must* believe these things in order to be accepted.

Jesus took a different approach. He called people to a way of life, not a creed. He said that the whole of religion could be summed up with these two basic requirements: to love God with all our heart, soul, mind and strength, and to love our neighbour as our self. The vast majority of his teaching can be read as an explanation of what these two requirements mean in practice. In theological jargon, Jesus focused on ortho*praxis* (getting our behaviour right) rather than ortho*doxy* (concern with believing the 'right' things).

According to John's Gospel, Jesus said, 'I am the way and the truth and the life. No one comes to the Father except through me.'* He did not, however, say that any particular dogma or creed was the way, the truth and the life, but that *he* was. He didn't say that we could 'come to the Father' by believing certain doctrines – even doctrines about him. He said that it was *through or by him* – by living, sharing in, being caught up by the Spirit that he embodied and expressed.

It is perfectly possible, therefore, to be in the way of Jesus without ever having heard of him or necessarily being persuaded by some of the things the Church teaches about him – just as it is completely possible for someone to experience God without being convinced that God exists. Beliefs are important, for sure, but faith is not primarily something in the head enclosed in words and concepts; it is more a fire in the belly, a gut instinct that we sense, which determines the way we live.

And surely it is the way we live that counts, much more than our theological beliefs. It puzzles me that people

---

* John 14:6.

sometimes try to judge whether I am a proper Christian by asking if I believe in certain things like the virgin birth, or the bodily resurrection of Jesus, or the authority of the Bible. Why don't they enquire how I treat my wife? Or ask what I spend my money on, or what I'm doing about injustice in the world? Why don't they ask whether I'm trying to care for God's Earth instead of simply adding to its problems? Surely these are the sorts of things that matter – not whether I mentally measure up to some notion of orthodoxy?

Faith, in fact, need not be defined or expressed in purely religious terms. Every one of us with even an ounce of spiritual intelligence experiences what Augustine refers to as a 'restless searching heart in the midst of a mysterious world'. We have an existential longing to know who we are, why we are here, what is the meaning of life, and how we are supposed to exist in the world. Faith, in its more generic sense, is a way of describing the way we go about processing these kinds of questions; it is our window on the world, our means of deciding what matters in life. Faith may be channelled through a particular religious tradition, but not necessarily. I know lots of people I would describe as people of faith who are not religious: people who are concerned with quality of life – their own and that of others. People who build their house on rock instead of sand, whose values, attitudes and practices affirm that life is more than selfish gain and pleasure, more than superficial existence. People who are caught up with things of ultimate concern.

I am therefore no longer interested in categorising folk simply on the basis of creed or religious affiliation. And I would find it impossible to believe in a God who would do that. Nowhere in the Gospels do we see Jesus requiring people to follow a creed or subscribe to a particular set of beliefs; his concern was with how they lived, how they handled money, how they treated others, what kind of choices they made. For Jesus, the kingdom of God wasn't an insurance policy for heaven when you die; it wasn't a religious system or an exclusive society. It was a clarion call to change the world by the power of God through compassion, healing, reconciliation and social justice. There was nothing to join, just a job to be done.

In psychological terms, faith is an exercise of the imagination, which is then lived out in the practicalities of life. It has its roots in the question 'what if . . .?' Faith is when we entertain (imagine, envisage, believe in) a different possibility, a different reality, and then start to live in the light of that. In essence, this is not a specifically religious process. It's a phenomenon supported by brain science, which tells us that the imagination can change the actual structure of the brain, and also lead to changes in external reality – because it changes the way we approach life, the sort of decisions we make, the course of actions we pursue.

Viktor Frankl was a Jewish psychiatrist who spent three years living in unspeakable horror in a Nazi concentration camp. While imprisoned, Frankl realised he had just one freedom left: the power to determine his response to his appalling situation. So he chose to imagine – to have faith. He imagined his wife and family members and the prospect of seeing them again. He imagined himself teaching his students after the war, handing on the lessons he had learned. And he did survive. Sadly, his wife was murdered by the Nazis, but he did indeed return to his work and went on to write many books, including his 1946 work *Man's Search for Meaning*, which sold more than 10 million copies.

Frankl's imagination wasn't a magic wand to guarantee a perfect outcome, but it enabled him to write a different story in his head to the one being imposed upon him by a ruthless regime of terror. And it preserved in him the will to outlive it. Frankl famously wrote, 'Everything can be taken from a man but one thing: the last of human freedoms – to choose one's attitude in any given set of circumstances, to choose one's own way.'

In the aftermath of the terrorist attack in Paris in 2015, dozens of stories of faith and courage were told. One that caught my eye occurred on a London tube train when a young man sat opposite a woman wearing a hijab. She smiled as he sat down. Then another man approached and began to abuse the Muslim woman, calling her things like 'raghead', 'terrorist' and 'scum', saying that her people murdered the victims in the Paris attack.

Without thinking, the young man stood to his feet and pushed the aggressor away, diverting the hostility towards himself. Shouted at and called a 'terrorist sympathiser', he sat next to the woman, who was in tears, and asked her name. Still barraged and threatened by verbal abuse, he distracted the woman, with small talk. When it got to his station, he asked if the woman would like him to stay with her until her stop. She thanked him for his 'tremendous kindness and bravery'. He didn't think he was being brave at all. 'I just saw someone in need,' he said, 'and it was my human nature to do what I could.'

At her stop, the young man escorted the woman off the train and up the escalator, where her friends met her. He gave her a hug and assured her that many people felt like him and that she shouldn't be afraid; this was her country, her city.

He didn't come across to me as especially religious, but he said that seeing her courage in being true to her beliefs even in the face of constant abuse inspired him to stand up for what he believed in – 'an equal, kind, and under-standing society despite religious and cultural differences'.

Constantly, we face the choice: whether to become more or less human. There can be no doubt which direc-tion the aggressive man chose that day on the tube. Yet those who stood by or looked away when the woman was abused sacrificed some little part of their humanity too. Of course, we all make bad choices. But the young man who stood up for the woman overcame fear to exercise faith, becoming more deeply human in the process. Instinctively, he reimagined the situation – 'how can I make this different?' – and then acted out what he imagined.

Each of us has an inner story, a narrative about ourselves and the world outside, which mostly remains fairly stable. Every day the story is reaffirmed through our attitudes and practices as well as through the expectations of people around us. Faith is when we change the story in a positive way that requires courage and resolve.

The young man on the train did not like the scenario he was a part of, even as a silent observer. Without any time to think it through, he launched himself into changing the narrative. He could not be sure how it would end, yet he committed himself to doing it anyway. He could have been beaten up, or even killed, but something more important than personal safety took over: a conviction that something had to be done. This is what I call an act of faith, regardless of whether religion played any explicit part in the process.

Faith is a (spiritual) muscle that can unleash change and transformation in the world. Any personal initiative or social movement that resists injustice or seeks goodness, beauty and liberation is faith-based in the most fundamental sense. It has to be; otherwise there would be no reason to hope for something better.

The arrival of fifteen young Muslims at our Midnight Mass, holding out hands for bread as a token of our common humanity, and receiving it, turned out to be a decisive symbol of hope to my neighbour – who longed for an expression of religion that acknowledged the importance of shades of grey in a world too often black and white.

3. I believe 'God' is just a word

what would happen if we dumped it?

*As soon as somebody tells you who God is ...
mistrust them!*

Lawrence Blair

What better way to spend an evening – an open-air concert with the incomparable Leonard Cohen? This was our third time in two years to see the veteran singer perform live. And being mid-July, I pictured us basking in the evening sun, savouring the golden voice of the man from Montreal, and sipping a glass or two of bubbly.

It didn't quite turn out that way. Grey clouds hung in the sky all day. Rain drizzled incessantly. The venue sat just a couple of miles from the motorway, but it took two and a half hours to get there, crawling through country lanes bumper to bumper. When we eventually arrived, having completely missed the support act, stewards armed with large sponges mopped the seats before we sat down.

Not a great start!

But our spirits were not to be dampened. We *are* British after all! A bit of rain wasn't going to spoil the fun.

As we settled into our seats Leonard Cohen was launching into his second song – 'There Ain't No Cure for Love'. Despite the inclement weather, he looked as dapper as ever: charcoal grey suit and trilby, with a scarf tied around his neck, and a voice 'deeper than a Siberian coalmine'. An exquisite choir of backing singers joined the ensemble of seasoned musicians from around the world.

But something was missing.

Atmosphere can be a fickle beast at open-air events. And I can't be sure whether it was the frustration people had experienced crawling through those country lanes, or the sound of trains whizzing along a line a couple of hundred yards behind the stage, or the discomfort of sitting on damp chairs in a chilly field, but the audience felt distracted, unfocused. The constant toing and froing of people shuffling to the hot dog stands, the beer tents and the toilets irritated the hell out of me. I wanted to bark at everyone who passed by.

Late in the evening Leonard Cohen introduced the Webb Sisters – two of the backing singers – to perform his song 'If It Be Your Will'. Graciously stepping aside, hat held to his chest, Cohen looked on like a doting father. Hattie and Charley Webb approached the microphones, one clasping a hand-held harp, the other a guitar.

I have always adored the song ('more of a prayer', Cohen says), which is based on the prayer of Jesus in the Garden of Gethsemane on the night of his arrest. It makes me cry every time I hear it. Leonard Cohen was once asked which song in the world he *wished* he had written. His response: ' "If It Be Your Will" . . . And I did.'

Almost as if preordained, during the opening bars of the song the weather changed. The heavens opened. No more drizzle. It bucketed down.

Possibly because of the rain, or in response to the two beautiful singers, or just because a crowd sometimes has a mind of its own, twelve thousand people spontaneously rose to their feet.

Suddenly, it was there – atmosphere by the cartload.

I'll be honest: I don't really like being rained on. I'm not that much of a hippie. Rain is something to look at through a window by a warm fire. But that night, with water babbling down my neck, drenched to my underwear, I didn't give a monkey's! In a flash I felt this weird sense of merging with everything – the crowd, the rain, the field, the music. I was consumed. There was no past, no future, just NOW. And from somewhere deep inside I heard a voice chanting, 'This is it! This is it!'

Something similar, if less intense, happened in the small valley in Yorkshire where we used to rent a hideaway cottage. It was late autumn, the atmosphere dull and leaden. While Pat prepared breakfast, I walked the dog up the valley. Then, out of nowhere, a gentle, dank mist descended. I could see almost nothing. All I heard was the sound of the stream and the plaintive cry of two buzzards echoing across the valley.

Pausing to get my bearings, I felt that same mysterious merging with everything. And to my amazement, I heard myself speaking in tongues out loud – something I hadn't done in years.* I have never felt more alive, more real, than in that moment.

---

* Speaking in tongues is a form of ecstatic speech practised in Charismatic and Pentecostal churches, which I had experienced in earlier days.

One other modest epiphany occurred, by contrast, in Florence while gazing at Michelangelo's statue of David. Surrounded by bustling sightseers, I just stood stock still staring at the figure for a full seven minutes. Far longer than I have spent in front of any other single piece of art.

I can't say why I was captivated. I didn't greatly ponder the statue as an object, or the biblical character it depicted. It wasn't like that. Actually, I didn't think about anything at all. I just stood there: breathtaken with wonder, but also strangely melancholic.

Weird as it may sound, if you ask me why I believe in God, I am far more inclined to recount one of these kinds of stories than to reel off some metaphysical or theological argument. Such incidents – and many others far more mundane – convince me that life is not just surface appearances, that there is a whole world of things beyond what we know with our senses. And this more than any rational argument supports my instinctive belief in God.

I am not discounting rational arguments; blind believism is a scourge on any religion and has nothing to do with faith. But experiences like the ones described shift the ground of the argument, opening up quite different possibilities for our notion of God.

The problem with most arguments for or against belief in God is that they tend to revolve around the same basic assumption: that 'God' means a human-like supreme being distinct from the universe, who made everything that is, who visited the world in Jesus, and who now occasionally intervenes in earthly affairs as 'he' sees fit. In very crude terms, this is what most people have in mind when they say 'God': believers and non-believers alike.

I took my leave of this God a long time ago, though it took a while to admit it. Back then my ministry was among churches where people believed that if you prayed long enough or hard enough, or if you mustered enough faith, you could expect God to intervene in some supernatural way. When that didn't happen, they would berate their lack of faith, or blame the devil for standing in the way of it, or decide that it wasn't God's will, or convince themselves that God had answered the prayer but in a different way. The whole thing was absurd to me. So I went in search of a different kind of religion, a different kind of God.

However, if the interventionist-style God is incredible to me, I equally cannot believe in the divine cosmic clockmaker, who created the universe, wound it up like a clock, then had no further involvement with it. This is a model of God that many scientists feel comfortable with. Stephen Hawking, for example, attributes the laws of physics to God in this way. He writes, 'These laws may have originally been decreed by God, but it appears that he has since left the universe to evolve according to them and does not intervene in it.'* Interestingly, Hawking's comment still seems to assume a supreme being, albeit a benevolent observer rather than one who interferes in earthly affairs. Yet I am no more interested in this God than I am in the interventionist equivalent. Why should I even care if such a God exists?

A faith that takes mystical experiences seriously leads to a very different way of thinking about God. Instead of a Supreme Being 'out there' (whether actively intervening in events, or setting things in motion then observing from a distance), we discover God in the depths of the material world, a God of dirt and passion, a pervading presence in everything, the energy that causes the universe to grow and evolve.

This is a God I don't simply believe in, but sense and experience every day, every moment: the breath of life in nature, the inspiration in human creativity, the bond of love between friends, the passionate impulse for justice and goodness in the world, the yearning to know and learn and explore. This is a God I can touch, and feel, and sense in the depth of my humanity.

---

* Stephen Hawking, *A Brief History of Time: From the Big Bang to Black Holes* (Bantam Books, 1988), p. 12.

I am not talking about pantheism; I don't see God and the universe as one and the same thing, any more than I see them as entirely separate. However, it is here in this world that I find God – in the magnificent creatures of Earth, in human companionship, in art and music and poetry, in the clumsiness of bodies entwined in passion, in the simple goodness of a loaf of bread, a glass of wine. Earth is crammed with divinity.

If we picture God as a boundless ocean in which the entire universe lives, then just as fish and other sea creatures cannot escape their watery home in the deep to discover an existence elsewhere, so we cannot escape God who is the home of creation, the matrix of all life, the one in whom 'we live and move and have our being'.* God doesn't intervene in our affairs like some outsider, but interacts with our lives in the same way that sea and fish combine and intermingle.

Unlike fish, however, we humans have the capacity to reflect on our place in the scheme of things, to wonder who and what we are and why we are here, to peek beyond the veil of routine existence and glimpse the greater whole. Mystical experiences are part of the 'peeking'.

I hope it is clear by now that when I speak of 'mystical experiences' I do not mean visions in the sky or

---

* Acts 17:28.

angels singing Handel's *Messiah* in the middle of the night, but something far more mundane. We all have little epiphanies, 'aha' moments, flashes of wonder and inspiration that help us to look at life, the world and ourselves in different ways. They may also help us to reimagine God.

Rabbi Lawrence Kushner says a mystic is 'anyone who has the gnawing suspicion that the apparent discord, brokenness, contradictions, and discontinuities that assault us every day might conceal a hidden unity'.* Which reminds me of the famous line from Leonard Cohen's song that says, 'There is a crack in everything; that's how the light gets in.'

In my experience, the spiritual juices really start to bubble up when we decide to follow the 'gnawing suspicion', when we pause to ponder the 'cracks', when we open up to the deeper dimension to things, the 'hidden unity' Rabbi Kushner speaks of, and try to explore what this means. In biblical language, 'hidden unity' means the fellowship of God's Spirit, but we can name it how we like. It isn't the words that matter but how we respond to the reality they signify.

---

* Rabbi Lawrence Kushner, *I'm God You're Not: Observations on Organized Religion and Other Disguises of the Ego* (Jewish Lights Publishing, 2010).

The problem in black and white approaches to religion is that God tends to be 'named' too confidently, too absolutely. Creeds and doctrines become literal facts instead of provisional attempts at truth. Then people behave as if they have a monopoly on God and truth, and anyone who disagrees is wrong. Yet surely humility alone tells us that God couldn't be ours; that what we discern of the divine is at best broken and limited, and prejudiced by our background and preconceptions.

All the great religious traditions acknowledge that God is a mystery beyond human comprehension; each has its own subtle methods for subverting black and white outcomes about who or what God is.

In Judaism the name of God quite literally cannot be uttered since it consists only of Hebrew vowels. If you try to speak the word, it (rather wonderfully) just makes the sound of breath.* In Islam, there can be no images or likenesses of God, human or otherwise; God cannot be pictured in any way. Hindus speak of 330 million gods, which for me is a way of saying that the names and dimensions to God are inexhaustible. Buddhists don't use 'God'

---

* In *The Book of Words*, Rabbi Lawrence Kushner insists that it is no coincidence that 'The holiest Name in the world, the name of the Creator, is the sound of your own breathing' (Jewish Lights Publishing, 2011), p. 28.

language, but point to the 'far shore', a reality that cannot be understood, but only experienced. Meanwhile, in Christianity, we have the mystery of the holy Trinity – one God in three persons – a conundrum that no one can begin to understand or explain.

God cannot be described without poetic licence. For, as St Paul writes, 'We don't yet see things clearly. We're squinting in a fog, peering through a mist.'* God is not literally a father with a son, a king, a shepherd or the Lord. These are mere metaphors, the language of poetry. Even the name 'God' is borrowed from paganism. Borrowed words are all we have to speak of God. As I heard someone say, God is always verbally dressed in second-hand clothes that don't fit very well.

However, none of this means that we cannot know or experience God. Early Christian thinkers stressed that while we can never get to the bottom of who or what God is *in essence*, we can nevertheless experience and know God through the expressions of divine energy in the world.

'Energy' is a wonderfully appropriate term to contemplate in connection with God, because like God energy is everywhere. It is the prime reality in the universe, the

---

* 1 Corinthians 13:12 (*The Message*).

foundation of everything from the minute atom to the mighty galaxy. Whether human, living, inorganic, stellar or atomic, everything is connected to everything else through energy. It is the great unifier in the cosmos. We cannot escape energy; we could well say that it is the reality in which we live and move and have our being.

If we think of the Big Bang at the creation of the universe as an explosion of divine energy, then the creation is a continuous bursting forth of God's Spirit. It is impossible to avoid God. In religious language, we could say that the universe is a divine sacrament, and every breath we draw, every step we take, every loaf of bread we eat, every hand offered in friendship should be received with gratitude as Holy Communion.

I never try to lead people to God. Introductions are not required. We all experience God in different ways, wittingly or unwittingly, by whatever name or description. However, my passion in life (I would say vocation) is helping people to sense the God already present with them and in them – the intimate stranger in the depths of their being.

I was recently invited to give a talk at the philosophy society in a London university college. My brief was to talk about religion and homosexuality – but with a philosophical twist! Relishing the opportunity, with a twinkle I announced my topic as 'I Met God, She's a Lesbian – Ontology for a Bad Christian'. Among other things, the talk focused on the many unexpected and perhaps shocking ways and forms in which God shows up in the world.

The following day I received several emails of appreciation. One that particularly interested me read, 'I've always thought of myself as an atheist. I don't like religion. And to be honest, I was shocked and not well pleased when I discovered a priest was talking to us. I thought we would get a sermon, and you'd try to make us join the church or something. But you shook me to my roots. I found myself agreeing with everything you said. If what you described really is God, then I'm not sure I can still call myself an atheist.'

The writer is far from alone; hordes of people abandon the idea of religion because the kind of faith – the kind of God – that they think is on offer appears implausible or repellent, if not utterly toxic, in a world where violence and terror are executed in God's name. Indeed, for many people, atheism is an ethical stance of protest against the things done in God's name.

In the mid-twentieth century, recognising the erosion of credibility in the name 'God', the theologian Paul Tillich proposed a moratorium on its use for at least one hundred years. It didn't happen, nor could it. But the point is well made: 'God' is probably the most used and abused word in history. Even as long ago as the thirteenth century, the Christian mystic Meister Eckhart exclaimed, 'I pray God to rid me of God!'

The question is: what on Earth do we mean by the word 'God'? My assumption is that, regardless of religious explanations, 'God' corresponds to something embedded in the deepest and truest aspects of our common human experience. For example, I see the human quest for things like ultimate beauty, truth and freedom as another way to describe the quest for God. Also, that when we experience unconditional love, we are encountering something utterly divine in nature and source.

So on one level, it doesn't matter whether or not we speak of 'God'. I may not know that there is something called 'the atmosphere', or I may call it something else, but that doesn't make the atmosphere unreal, or stop me from experiencing it every moment. God-talk is deeply problematic for some people. I myself find it problematic when I hear and see the way it is used. Yet I am convinced that in its stammering way 'God' does point to a reality universally experienced in some fashion, something at the core of our existence.

At its best, religion is not only a way of naming the mystery at the heart of the universe (a naming which, incidentally, should be under constant review) but also a confident path of engagement with it. For me, the Christian tradition offers a community of shared speech and symbols that enables me to explore and celebrate the mystery of God. And in Jesus I find the most compelling embodiment of that mystery in human form.

I also find in Christianity a vigorous forum of debate and disagreement. For me, tradition should never become a closed system of belief, a community of conformity, but a heated debate, a place of relentless, billowing diversity. I am part of this tradition, but I hope always to be a black sheep within it, constantly questioning, constantly rethinking, constantly opening myself to fresh insights, fresh experiences.

At the end of the day, 'God' is a makeshift term, a stop-gap: a way of clearing the throat (as Leonard Cohen might say) before attempting, once again, to utter the unutterable.

4. I believe in poetry, art and rock'n'roll
did God write any good tunes lately?

There'll always be religion around while there is poetry.

Les Murray

On the evening of 12 October 1931, the jazz musician Louis Armstrong opened a three-day run at the Driskill Hotel in Austin, Texas. In the crowd that night was a college student named Charlie Black. He knew nothing of jazz. Hadn't even heard of Louis Armstrong. He just reckoned there would be lots of girls to dance with.

Then the great man began to play.

Charlie recalled the experience years later:

Steam-whistle power, lyric grace, alternated at will, even blended. Louis played mostly with his eyes closed; just before he closed them they seemed to have ceased to look outward, to have turned inward, to the world out of which the music was to flow . . . letting flow from that inner space of music, things that had never before existed.*

Louis Armstrong was the first genius Charlie ever encountered. And he was black. The significance of this for a sixteen-year-old Southern boy at that time cannot be overstated. He had literally never seen a black person in anything but a servant's capacity.

Charlie went on to become a towering figure in the world of constitutional law and civil rights, serving on the legal team that won 'Brown versus the Board of Education' – the landmark case that abolished segregated education in the United States.

But he never forgot where it all began:

---

* Taken from Charles L. Black, 'My World With Louis Armstrong', http://bit.ly/1KWOZ83.

Through many years now, I have felt that it was just then [hearing Louis Armstrong play] that I started walking toward the Brown case, where I belonged . . . Louis opened my eyes wide, and put to me a choice. Blacks, the saying went were 'all right in their place.' But what was the 'place' of such a man, and of the people from which he sprang?

On 17 May 1954, state laws upholding segregated public schools for black and white students were abolished. It was the beginning of the end of the old Southern racist regime.

Following the Supreme Court verdict, a black community organisation held a reception at the Harlem Savoy Ballroom in honour of the lawyers who had worked on the case. Charlie's wife Barbara gazed at her husband with pride when it came to his turn: 'And next over there is Charlie Black, a white man from Texas who's been with us all the way.' For Charlie, this had long ago ceased to be a fight for justice for somebody else. This was *his* battle for and with *his* people.

Later, after the party, the couple stood silently in their apartment living room. Charlie went over to the record player and put on Louis Armstrong's 'Savoy Blues', which they listened to all the way through without exchanging a word. In that one record he always felt he heard something said: a voice 'neither strident nor self-pitying' saying something like, 'We are being wronged; grievously, heavily, bewilderingly wronged. We don't know why, or what to do. Is anyone listening? Is there anyone to come and help us?' Then the gentle coda: 'I leave it up to you.'

For Charlie, Louis Armstrong's music was 'religion in art', through which he received a call every bit as compelling and significant as the voice Moses heard from the burning bush in the wilderness. Moses went on to lead the children of Israel out of slavery in Egypt; Charlie Black confronted his own race, his own class and social circle, to help bring down America's 'caste system' of racial segregation.

He had attended a jazz concert hoping to dance with some girls, and ended up stumbling on a treasure beyond price. Something 'inexhaustible' and 'unknowable', which took hold of his life and he never turned back.

The quest for ultimate beauty, like the quest for ultimate truth or ultimate love, is really a quest for God by whatever name, and all genuine art is pregnant with divine revelation, regardless of its subject matter or the artist's religious disposition. Divinity gestates in the creative imagination, waiting to materialise in human experience in a million different ways. As Pope John Paul II writes in his *Letter to Artists*, 'every true art form in its own way is a path to the inmost reality of humanity and the world. This reality is God.'

Traditionally, Western Christianity has been preoccupied with understanding God through conceptual and rational terms – through beliefs, doctrines and creeds. These are undoubtedly significant. Yet a purely rational, verbalised faith is a miserably impoverished one.

My assumption is that all human beings have within them something the Quakers call 'the inner light', a non-rational, non-verbal awareness of the mystery of God, and that the arts are an essential means to experience and express that awareness. Whether through paintings, sculpture, writing, theatre, dance, rock'n'roll, or indeed a jazz musician's trumpet, art gives vent to the haunted human longing for mystery. Indeed, all genuine art ultimately draws us towards that reality.

Certainty, on the other hand, is the enemy of both true art and true religion. It brings false closure to what never can be resolved. Though they are different things, art and religion share the common purpose of subverting certainties and drawing us to the edge of mystery. Without a sense of the mysterious, art degenerates into chocolate-box romanticism, or propaganda; religion becomes hollow ritual, or dogmatic fundamentalism.

Not that mystery is invariably comforting; sometimes it may be deeply disturbing and challenging. As the graffiti artist Banksy famously commented, art should comfort the disturbed and disturb the comfortable. The same is true of religion. Which is why the dark night of the soul is such a vital part of Christian spirituality, the disruption of false certitude, the retaining of mystery.

In his poem *Self-Portrait*, David Whyte discards the superficial reassurances of religious identity and God-talk. The answers provided in them are unimportant; the questions raised are hardly worth asking. Instead, the poem exposes the grand mystery inherent in the human condition, regardless of culture or creed, and poses questions definitely worth asking – chiefly: do we have the honesty to face the yearning that is deep inside the human soul, the courage to live in the truest sense? The poem isn't disinterested in the matter of God, but reaches for 'the God beyond God', as Paul Tillich puts it, the reality to which our God-talk points but which it never can contain.

> **Self-Portrait**
> It doesn't interest me if there is one God
> or many gods.
> I want to know if you belong or feel
> abandoned,

If you know despair or can see it in others.
I want to know
if you are prepared to live in the world
with its harsh need
to change you. If you can look back
with firm eyes,
saying this is where I stand. I want to know
if you know
how to melt into that fierce heat of living,
falling toward
the center of your longing. I want to know
if you are willing
to live, day by day, with the consequence of love
and the bitter
unwanted passion of your sure defeat.

I have been told, in *that* fierce embrace, even
the gods speak of God.*

Despite being a lifelong church member and a priest for
many years, some of my best encounters with God have
not been in religious services and activities, but in art

---

* David Whyte, *Self-Portrait*, from *Fire in the Earth* (Many Rivers
Press, 1992), and *River Flow: New and Selected Poems* (Many Rivers
Press, 2012). Used by permission.

galleries, theatres, cinemas, concerts and poetry books. The writer John O'Donohue remarks that some of his best friends are poems. And I would say that some of my most profound encounters with God have been in poems, songs and other works of art.

In September 2012, my wife and I joined a capacity crowd at Battersea Arts Centre in London for a performance by the poet and rapper Kate Tempest. Dubbed the laureate of south-east London street life, Tempest delivers a unique blend of poetry, rap and storytelling with all the passion and conviction of a street-preaching evangelist.

Described as a secular sermon, *Brand New Ancients* is a modern-day parable of two south London families, which reveals that the world of the old gods is not so far from our world – the old myths still continue in our 'everyday odysseys' of violence, bravery, sacrifice and love. Divinity is ever present in our tense, broken, screwed-up world and lives.

Kate Tempest's *Brand New Ancients* is a summons to arms, a wake-up call to the significance and wonder in humdrum existence.

> We have jealousy
> and tenderness and curses and gifts.
> But the plight of a people who have forgotten their
>   myths

and imagine that somehow now is all that there is
is a sorry plight,
all isolation and worry –
but the life in your veins
it is godly, heroic.
You were born for greatness;
believe it. Know it.
Take it from the tears of the poets.

There's always been heroes
and there's always been villains
and the stakes may have changed
but really there's no difference.
There's always been greed and heartbreak and
    ambition
and bravery and love and trespass and contrition –
we're the same beings that began, still living
in all of our fury and foulness and friction,
everyday odysseys, dreams and decisions . . .
The stories are there if you listen.

The stories are here,
the stories are you,
and your fear
and your hope

is as old
as the language of smoke,
the language of blood,
the language of
languishing love.*

I wept and laughed my way through the evening. Afterwards, as she signed my copy of her book, I said to Kate, 'I am a vicar, and I want to tell you – that was possibly the best fricking sermon I have ever heard!' And it was.

I left Battersea Arts Centre challenged, blessed and invigorated – feeling far more alive than when I went in. It wasn't a religious event, and yet it was deeply religious. With poetry, music and gut-wrenching humanity, Kate Tempest pointed us towards the mystery and wonder of life. Towards God, I'd say.

The claim that art may be an authentic source of divine revelation, equally as powerful and compelling as any religious text, will be shocking – maybe blasphemous – to some traditional Christians. For them, the Bible is the Word of God, the only true and reliable source of divine truth. I am very familiar with this point of view; I grew up with it.

---

* Kate Tempest, *Brand New Ancients* (Picador, 2013). © Kate Tempest. Used by permission.

Yet even as a teenager I found it puzzling that we could be so sure that the Bible was 'written' by God; that this text more than any other was 'the Word of God'. The answer I received – 'because that's what the Bible tells us' – struck me as ... well ... daft, really. I also couldn't understand why God would 'write' only one book. I even facetiously asked my youth leader if God got writer's block after finishing the Bible. Well, it was at that point that I discovered the limits of my youth leader's sense of humour.

The Bible actually enjoyed such high regard in my church that even when a copy was bruised and battered and falling to pieces through overuse, no one could quite bring themselves to throw it away. The normal practice, so far as I could tell, was to retire old Bibles to a quiet, dignified spot on a bookshelf (some people had quite a few); although I do recall one man saying he had buried his old Bible at the bottom of the garden in a shoebox. I am not sure if he said a prayer or gave a eulogy!

The near deification of the Bible that I grew up with was extreme, but actually, many Christians take the view that the Good Book is either literally God's Word, or contains words directly inspired by God in a way that no other book does, and that this gives it a unique authority.

I love the Bible. I read it most days of my life; I teach it and preach on it almost every week. It is the matrix from which my faith has emerged and which still provides much of the grammar for my religious experience. However, the idea that this one book could be the exclusive and definitive Word of God is something I find incredible. How could the exuberant, creative Spirit of the universe, the sacred presence in everything, be revealed only in the Bible – and in the community that reveres it (which happens to be ours)? This is a belief that can only make sense to those who are immersed in the Christian ghetto; anyone who has really looked outside that ghetto cannot possibly accept it.

The Bible is a human book, *and none the worse for that*. Written over a period of around 1,500 years, it is the product of two historical communities, the ancient Hebrews and the early Christians, and reveals how these communities knew and understood God and practised their faiths. The Bible is a culturally conditioned text: it arises out of particular social settings and reflects the historical insights of the time.

Even though some people will hear this as a very negative view of the Bible, it really isn't. Nor does it in any way undermine the Bible's unique, though not exclusive, capacity to reveal God in powerful and transformative ways today. But recognising the humanity of the book enables us to read it critically as well as humbly – to recognise its limitations as well as exposing ourselves to its truth.

Some parts of the Bible I find ceaselessly inspiring and challenging – for example, passages like Jesus' Sermon on the Mount or Paul's hymn to love in 1 Corinthians 13, to name just two. Other parts I find abhorrent and will oppose and challenge tenaciously – much of the book of Joshua, for example, which pictures God supporting and even commissioning genocide as the rampaging Israelites exterminate the Canaanites in a fashion we might now expect from a group like ISIS; also passages where women are presumed to be inferior to men, or where slavery is sanctioned.

Reading the Bible in a literal fashion leaves any openminded reader with all kinds of problems. If we believe, for instance, that God is all good and all loving, then how can we excuse 'his' appalling behaviour in sending plagues on innocent Egyptians simply because they had a stubborn, cruel leader? Or how can we explain God turning the life of his faithful servant Job into a living hell just because of some apparent wager with Satan?

How are we in a scientific age to believe that a cloud carried Jesus into the heavens, or that the world was made in six days?

Not only does a literal interpretation of the Bible beggar belief in today's world, it is also bad reading practice. The truth or wisdom of a text does not depend upon its factuality. We don't read poetry to discover scientific data, or look at a Picasso to see a mirror image of the person painted. Similarly, the impact a novel or a film can have on our life is not dependent on the story being a 'real-life' account. The only important question is: what does this poem, picture, story mean? What does it tell us about the world, or about the human condition, or about our life? What questions does it raise? What journey does it open up? And so on. To the creative imagination, truth is more holistic than a bald fact can ever convey. It explores the interior of things, not just the outward surface.

The ancient idea of wisdom offers a more biblical way of understanding the meaning of truth. According to the Greeks, wisdom is the love of the highest things – the true, the good and the beautiful. It includes the rational and the factual, but goes far beyond that; it has aesthetic and ethical dimensions too.

I see the natural language of the Bible, of religion in

general, to be poetic and metaphorical. Here, wisdom has room to breathe. We should not come to the Bible looking for scientifically or historically sustainable facts, but for truth in this greater sense: as wisdom for living a good and beautiful life. Once we embrace this, many of the problems people have with the Bible disappear, and we can expose ourselves to what it has to say – bask in its truth – without stretching credulity to breaking point.

Has God written any good tunes lately? Yes, of course. But you won't necessarily hear them in church (though you might). Wherever I look in the world I discover divine revelation – at a music gig or on iTunes, in a poetry book or an art gallery, on TV or at the theatre, in the playfulness of a child or the liberated imagination of a grown-up. It enriches my life, and sometimes calls me to a different life, as it did Charlie Black when he heard Louis Armstrong.

I fell in love with the music of Nick Cave when my daughter-in-law Cyndi played me one of his songs. He has inspired me ever since. He admits, 'If I am a Christian, I am a very bad one.' Yet he also states that there are only two things he cares about in the world: love and God. And despite starting one of his songs with the line 'I don't believe in an interventionist God', he clearly understands

God to be a real, living entity with whom we can have a meaningful relationship.*

In a fascinating lecture entitled 'The Flesh Made Word', Cave argues eloquently that the medium through which this interaction occurs is the creative imagination. At one point it may sound as if he is saying that God is nothing more than the invention of the imagination: 'There is a God. God is the product of the creative imagination, and God is that imagination taken flight.'† However, this is easily misread. It is not in question for Cave that there is a God, or that we can have a meaningful relationship with God; his concern is with how the encounter occurs. The thrust of his conclusion is that it is through the creative process – 'the imagination taken flight' – that we experience God.

This idea of the imagination taken flight equates fully with my understanding of the nature of faith. Faith is essentially an activity of the imagination, an exercise in 'what if-ness', which makes room for a different reality to take form in our experience. Few things evoke that faith

* For an excellent discussion of Nick Cave's approach to faith, see Anna Kessler, 'Faith, Doubt, and the Imagination: Nick Cave on the Divine-Human Encounter', in Michael J. Gilmour (ed.), *Call Me the Seeker: Listening to Religion in Popular Music* (Continuum, 2005).
† Nick Cave, 'The Flesh Made Word', originally written for BBC Radio 3, broadcast in 1996.

in me more effectively than expressions of the creative process, which prompt direct access to the imagination and 'ultimately to God'.

Nick Cave maintains that all true love songs are directed, in the end, to God, hence: 'the actualising of God through the medium of the love song remains my prime motivation as an artist'.

I believe (and discover in practice) that poetry, art and rock'n'roll – the entire gamut of the creative arts – contain the potentiality to connect me to the God I find in Jesus Christ.

5. I believe in evolution, and the Big Bang
and other creation myths

The Big Bang is our modern scientific creation myth; it comes from the same human need to solve the cosmological riddle (Where did the universe come from?).

Carl Sagan

I will never forget that crisp Yorkshire night when Pat and I left a warm cottage and a blazing log fire to stand in the middle of a frozen field and look up at the starlit sky.

Where we live in London you don't really get to see the night sky; cities are awash with artificial light, masking out all but the brightest of stars. But as we stood in that valley three miles from the nearest street-lamp, the dazzling splendour of the starry heavens hung above us like a vast, looming presence, silent and still.

After looking up for a few moments I surrendered to a visceral urge to lie on my back on the hard, frosty earth and gaze at the Milky Way – billions of stars merged in a swathe of freckled light. It almost felt like I was staring into the face of God.

How could I begin to comprehend the immense distances stretched out before me? Even the nearest star is four light years away (approximately 24 trillion miles). The pinprick of light from the galaxy Andromeda, which we can just about detect with the naked eye, began its journey to Earth 2.5 million years ago. I was literally peering through history, across eons of time and space. Little wonder I shuddered with that mental vertigo I first sensed as a child when I lay in a dark bedroom trying to imagine eternity.

I have always been fascinated by the heavens. When I was about twelve I sent a five-shilling postal order to the Royal Astronomical Society to purchase a map of the moon. And I swapped my bike for a friend's telescope.

My dad wasn't impressed, but I was ecstatic and couldn't wait for nightfall. For hours I would lie on the tin roof of our back-yard shed scanning the lunar landscape, or squinting at the stars, trying to spot which of them were planets.

The thing that struck me back then, and which has never left me since, is the sense that we are all part of this vast, cosmic adventure: the history of the universe is written in our DNA, woven into the very fabric of our being. As Joni Mitchell's song says, 'We are stardust: billion-year-old carbon'* – weirdly and wonderfully fashioned into living souls with the capacity to think and reflect on who and what we are. In the mind-boggling words of the cosmologist Carl Sagan, 'The nitrogen in our DNA, the calcium in our teeth, the iron in our blood, the carbon in our apple pies were made in the interiors of collapsing stars. We are made of starstuff.' And we have evolved into sentient beings who now seek to understand the universe: 'We are a way for the universe to know itself.'†

In 1859 Darwin's *Origin of Species* presented the theory of biological evolution, a system of understanding human history right back to its prehistoric roots. Now, scientists

* From Joni Mitchell, 'Woodstock' (1969).
† Carl Sagan, *Cosmos* (Abacus, 1983).

have expanded the storyline back to the beginning of time, to the Big Bang and the origins of the universe itself. We now understand that the universe is not a settled entity but a process: less of a 'thing' and more of an 'event'. The cosmos is a story of *becoming*. We are part of that becoming, part of the unfolding drama of cosmic evolution. Nothing is a finished entity. The whole of creation is on a voyage of discovery.

According to present estimates, the universe story began around 14 billion years ago with the Big Bang – a term that is itself a metaphor since there wasn't really an explosion in any sense we can understand. It wasn't a case of matter exploding into empty space, but space itself expanding very rapidly. It's a concept most of us can't even begin to comprehend. As the expansion took place, the solar system was formed around 4.6 billion years ago, with the Earth evolving from clouds of dust and gases left over from the creation of the sun.

In its earliest times, planet Earth was a cauldron of roiling molten rock, mercilessly bombarded with meteorites and other celestial debris. Eventually, after millennia, it cooled and developed an outer crust; the first solid rocks were formed. There were no continents, just a mighty ocean dotted with small islands. Through erosion, sedimentation and volcanic activity, small continents appeared which grew until they reached roughly their present size 2.5 billion years ago.

During a gradual mutation taking somewhere between 200 and 600 million years, life forms evolved from microbes to cells to organisms. This opens up one of the great mysteries of cosmic evolution: how it all happened, how lifeless chemicals floating around aimlessly for eons of time suddenly erupted into life. Also, was it a one-off occurrence, or did something similar happen elsewhere in the universe? Are there other beings far, far away, gazing across space through telescopes, wondering if there is life out there? We still cannot say, though I find it inconceivable that the voluptuous creator of this verdant little planet, teeming with life, would not also give birth to other equally swarming worlds of existence. Surely we cannot be the one and only bright bauble in God's universe.

Only in the last 570 million years did the kind of life forms we are familiar with begin to evolve on Earth, starting with invertebrates, then fish, land plants and forests. Mammals evolved just 200 million years ago. Homo sapiens appeared a mere 200,000 years ago.

Questions about the origins of the universe have puzzled the human imagination from its inception. Where did everything come from? How did creation happen?

Why are we here? And so, in the absence of anything like a factual account of cosmic beginnings, we told stories, creation myths, sacred narratives to explain how the world was formed, where human life began.

The creation myth I grew up with is written in the opening chapters of Genesis in the Bible. Of course, I never thought of it as a myth. I learned it as a child and assumed it to be literally true: that God really did make the world in six days, that the human race sprang from two ancestors, Adam and Eve, who ate the forbidden fruit and ended up being expelled from the Garden of Eden.*

No one told me that other religions, other cultures, had their own creation stories, which would naturally appear equally true to them as Genesis did to me. Only at school, studying biology, and hearing about prehistoric animals, fossils and the theory of evolution, did the first doubts enter my mind about the factuality of Genesis. But even then it took years to undo the simplistic acceptance of the story instilled in me as a child.

Part of my process of rethinking was the discovery of other creation myths from different parts of the world that fascinated me, not because I imagined them to be

---

* Genesis 1 and 2 basically constitute different creation accounts; confusingly, the second is actually the older version. But for the sake of what I am writing here, I am bunching the two together.

literally true but because they are such wonderful stories, and magnificent repositories of wisdom from those traditions.

Nowadays the term 'myth' tends to be taken as simply meaning something that is untrue, but properly speaking a myth is a literary device, a story that is told over and over through successive generations to explain why things are the way they are. Their influence has been and still is enormous. The historian Karen Armstrong says that myths are 'universal and timeless stories that reflect and shape our lives – they explore our desires, our fears, our longings, and provide narratives that remind us what it means to be human'.*

Armstrong insists that it was never intended for creation myths to be taken as historically accurate; that isn't the point. Indeed, the very notion of history and historical accuracy is itself a quite modern idea. In ancient cultures people were less concerned with historical fact than with wisdom: a story was true if it was regarded as reliable and sage; if it offered guidance, direction or enlightenment. Most importantly, a creation myth was seen to be true because it formed part of that people's tradition, because it was how *they* saw things as a community, how they understood the world and themselves.

---

* Karen Armstrong, *A Short History of Myth* (Canongate Books, 2005).

Universally, creation stories convey the sense that the Earth does not belong to us; that we are players in a greater drama, with an implied accountability for the way we treat the Earth and its creatures, for the way we live our lives.

The ancient creation myth symbolises an age of ecological innocence, when humans knew and accepted their place in the web of life: when people worked in partnership with nature instead of treating it as a utility, or seeing it as a separate entity. For the ancients, the world was a place of enchantment: a place where rocks, trees, rivers and clouds were wondrous and alive, where creation was filled with mystery, evoking wonder and reverence. People lived with what Morris Berman calls a 'participating consciousness' – a sense of belonging in the world, of belonging *to* the world, of *being* the world. There was no world/us differentiation.*

St Francis of Assisi encapsulates this participating consciousness with his 'Canticle of the Sun' in which even 'Sister Death' has her place in the great household of creation:

Most high, all powerful, all good Lord!
All praise is Yours, all glory, all honour, and all
blessing.

---

* Morris Berman, *The Re-enchantment of the World* (Cornell University Press, 1981).

I believe in evolution, and the Big Bang

To You, alone, Most High, do they belong.
No mortal lips are worthy to pronounce Your name.

Be praised, my Lord, through all Your creatures,
especially through my lord Brother Sun,
who brings the day; and You give light through him.
And he is beautiful and radiant in all his splendour!
Of You, Most High, he bears the likeness.

Be praised, my Lord, through Sister Moon and the
    stars;
in the heavens You have made them bright, precious
    and beautiful.

Be praised, my Lord, through Brothers Wind and Air,
and clouds and storms, and all the weather,
through which You give Your creatures sustenance.

Be praised, my Lord, through Sister Water;
she is very useful, and humble, and precious, and
    pure.

Be praised, my Lord, through Brother Fire,
through whom You brighten the night.
He is beautiful and cheerful, and powerful and strong.

Be praised, my Lord, through our sister Mother
    Earth,
who feeds us and rules us,
and produces various fruits with coloured flowers
    and herbs.

Be praised, my Lord, through those who forgive for
    love of You;
through those who endure sickness and trial.

Happy those who endure in peace,
for by You, Most High, they will be crowned.

Be praised, my Lord, through our sister Bodily
    Death,
from whose embrace no living person can escape.
Woe to those who die in mortal sin!
Happy those she finds doing Your most holy will.
The second death can do no harm to them.

Praise and bless my Lord, and give thanks,
and serve Him with great humility.*

---

* St Francis of Assisi, 'Canticle of the Sun', trans. Bill Barrett, in
Katherine Paterson, *Brother Sun, Sister Moon* (Chronicle Books,
2011).

This era of ecological naivety predominated in the West right up to the eve of the scientific revolution, but finally the Enlightenment and the Industrial Revolution together fashioned a new consciousness, a different story: *the myth of human individuality and human progress*, with its illusion that technology and science could create the prosperity for which we longed.

Fired by this new narrative, we humans in the West have been on a centuries-long rampage of conquering, plundering, exploiting and polluting the planet. No longer sensing that the natural world and its creatures are kith and kin, we have become estranged overlords in creation, bending and fashioning it to our will and purpose.

The outcome of our new 'relationship' with the Earth is proving disastrous, with climate change, species depletion and widespread destruction of the biosphere. The likelihood now is that climate change will continue through this century and beyond; temperatures will continue to increase, there will be more droughts and heat waves, hurricanes will become stronger and more intense, sea levels will continue to rise, and in a matter of decades the Arctic will very likely become ice free during the summer months.

Faced with the catastrophe of rising sea levels, displaced communities, habitat destruction, loss of secure sources of food and clean water, the veteran environmental activist and writer Joanna Macy describes three contemporary stories, or versions of reality, each of which serves as a lens through which to see and understand what is going on.*

In the first scenario, *Business as Usual*, the defining assumption is that we have virtually no need to change anything at all; we simply carry on as we are. Economic growth and technological advancement remain the essential priorities in this story, and the central plot is about getting ahead. Those who point to the damage we are causing to the environment (as well as to the poor of the world) and call for a change in priorities and lifestyle are labelled prophets of doom, to be ignored and marginalised. And anyway, even if there is an ecological crisis, technology and economic progress will provide the solution. There is no need to worry.

The second story, *the Great Unravelling*, is the version of reality emerging from virtually every credible scientific source in the world, and from conservationists like David Attenborough, who, far from being prophets of doom, are lovers of the world, but also troubled observers of what they see happening to it. The Great Unravelling

---

* See Joanna Macy and Molly Brown, *Coming Back to Life* (New Society Publishers, 2014).

draws attention to the disasters that Business as Usual is causing, and has already caused. It is an account of things supported by vast swathes of evidence from around the world. It is the alarm bell that warns, 'Something is going horribly wrong!' Understandably, this isn't a message most of us wish to hear.

The third story acknowledges the reality of the Great Unravelling but refuses to let it have the last word. It's a story of hope and redemption, but also of challenge, which requires a change from Business as Usual to a more sustainable way of life where the Earth and its biosphere have the chance to recover from our devastating policies and practices. Joanna Macy calls this story *the Great Turning*, a title which corresponds closely with what the New Testament calls 'repentance': the willingness to shift into a new and larger mindset – a mentality of compassion, healing and justice for all creation.

All three of these stories are happening, right now. The question is, which will we choose to support, to put our energy into? It is clear that, short of becoming hermits, none of us in the West can entirely extricate ourselves from the culture of Business as Usual; the very infrastructure of our lives is rooted in that version of reality. Yet this cannot be a reason to do nothing. There are choices we can make, options we can select, many of which are inconvenient and painful, yet utterly necessary.

Stephen Hawking comments that we are at the most dangerous moment in the development of humanity, when we desperately need to work together to face our awesome environmental challenges: climate change, food production, overpopulation, the decimation of species, epidemic disease, acidification of the oceans. Without question, this issue of the devastation of the environment is by far the biggest and most urgent problem facing the human race. Yet governments and financial institutions remain locked solidly into the narrative and priorities of Business as Usual.

The myth of *human individuality and human progress* has landed us in a devastating mess. We need a different story to live by, a shift of consciousness that restores the sense of being part of the Earth community, the realisation that what we do to the Earth we do to ourselves. We have outgrown the old creation myths, but the narrative that replaced them is wreaking havoc on the Earth and threatening our very future as a species.

We need a new sacred story which enables us to live with the planet, with the entire Earth community, in a mutually beneficial way: a story which is rooted in the vision of the Earth and the universe given to us by science and cosmology, but which also validates the earlier stories that generate the sense of a sacred cosmos.

To make progress with this, we must first set aside the ridiculous idea that science and faith are intrinsically in conflict with each other. At the one extreme, *scientism* insists that only scientific knowledge is worth anything and spurns religious perception as superstition. At the other extreme, *creationism* discards the scientific theory of evolution and clings to a literal interpretation of the creation narratives in Genesis. Both extremes fall headlong into a category mistake: the Genesis creation narratives are poetic in nature, not scientific. They each strive for truth, but in different ways.

As we stand, the new story of creation that is being told across the world is that of cosmic and biological evolution. Parts of the story may change. Perhaps some bits will be shown to be wrong. But this is by far the best story we have of how the universe, the Earth and human life came into being. It is told in schools and universities by scientists, but also on TV by great scientific storytellers like Brian Cox and David Attenborough, whose documentaries unfold the magnificence of the world and the universe. But the story also needs to be told in churches by clergy and others unafraid to configure science and faith as two halves of a whole picture.

> Tell me a story more wondrous than that of a living cell forged from the residue of exploding stars. Tell me a story of transformation more magical than that of a fish hauling out onto land and becoming amphibian, or a reptile taking to the air and becoming a bird, or a mammal slipping back into the sea and becoming a whale.
>
> Connie Barlow*

Michael Dowd, a popular science writer, helpfully differentiates between what he calls 'Day' language and 'Night' language. Day language is the language we use to describe facts or things which we believe are objectively real and provable; it's the natural idiom of science or history and employs terms which are factual and accurate. Night language, on the other hand, is the language we use to describe things which are more subjective, less verifiable, yet nonetheless real; it's the natural language of poetry, art and mystery, but also of religion, and finds expression in grand metaphors, symbols and vibrant images.

Earlier creation myths were essentially 'night' stories, not attempting to meet modern criteria of factuality or

---

* Connie Barlow, *Green Space, Green Time: The Way of Science* (Springer-Verlag, 1997).

objectivity. Yet they offered truthful accounts of the world as people experienced it, and served as timeless guides in navigating the joys and hazards of everyday life. Today, religion and spirituality can still offer useful 'night-time' lenses to supplement and interpret the 'day-time' language of science as we seek to formulate creation stories to live by.

For me, God is a mysterious presence embedded in the universe; so much so that the process of cosmic, biological and human evolution is actually part of the story of God. I do believe that God is more than the universe, but I see the universe as the closest thing that God has to a body. Therefore, what happens to the universe or, more pertinently, to the world, in some way also happens to God. The joys and sufferings of the world are the joys and sufferings of God. And when I gazed at the Milky Way on that icy night and felt I was gazing into the face of God, in a way I was.

The stories we desperately need today are stories of belonging: of humans belonging to the Earth, of sensing a common history with the planet, of feeling empathy with Brother Sun, Sister Moon and Mother Earth, of deep realisation that what we do to our creaturely kith and kin we also do to ourselves.

I find it interesting that the language of almost every astronaut who has looked back on the Earth from space borders on the religious: the Earth is a 'holy relic', 'a small pearl in a thick sea of mystery', something 'small and blue and beautiful' floating in 'eternal silence', 'a beautiful, warm, living object'. But I am also struck by the sense of belonging that was generated: of deep affinity with something that was awesome but fragile and needing to be respected and cared for.

In 1948, the British astronomer Fred Hoyle anticipated this response when he said that once a photograph of the Earth (taken from outside) became available, a new idea as powerful as any in history would be let loose. We would be able to see ourselves in a new light. Well, now we have those photographs. And the 'blue marble' image of the Earth shot from the moon has become an icon of our times – a visual psalm of praise.

A new story of creation is emerging: a blend of science, poetry and spiritual insight, of 'day' and 'night' language. We are part of the magnificent adventure of cosmic and biological evolution, which is also the story of God's love affair with the world and the universe. In cosmological terms, the whole of humanity, past, present and future, is a speck on a speck on a speck on a speck – a microscopic footnote in a story too vast to comprehend. Yet when we open our hearts and minds to the looming, mysterious presence that I sensed lying in a frosty field in Yorkshire, we can somehow know that our little lives mean something. And like David, the ancient king of Israel who started life as a shepherd boy, also lying in a field three thousand years before me, gazing at the same Milky Way, we declare:

> When I gaze to the skies and meditate on Your
>   creation—
> on the moon, stars, *and all* You have made,
> I can't help but wonder why You care about mortals—
> sons *and daughters* of men—
> *specks of dust floating about the cosmos.**

---

* Psalm 8:3–4 (*The Voice*).

6. I believe in original goodness
we enter the world in a state of grace

God saw all that he had made, and it was very
good.

Genesis 1:31

I am good, but not an angel. I do sin, but I am not
the devil. I am just a small girl in a big world trying
to find someone to love.

Marilyn Monroe

James was a murderer. I never knew the circumstances of his crime; just that he suffered from mental illness. The court committed him to a psychiatric hospital, where he spent twelve years before being moved to a facility in my parish, to be rehabilitated into the community.

People loved James. He was warm, funny and engaging, and he appeared to be making great progress. Then one day, to everyone's disbelief, he went into a tube station, threw himself under a moving train, and was killed instantly.

James's family had disowned him after the trial. No one but his beloved sister Karen visited him in hospital. They weren't biological siblings, both were adopted as babies, but a deep bond existed between them. Karen never lost sight of the man she always knew James to be.

At the funeral she spoke movingly about her brother, and ended the eulogy with Adele's cover version of the Bob Dylan track 'Make You Feel My Love'. Mostly, I hold it together at a funeral (no one needs a blubbing vicar!), but on this occasion I made an exception. There was something very pure and defiant about Karen's love for James, which the song encapsulated beautifully. She really would have held him for a million years if he'd let her, but in the end he slipped beyond even her grip.

Apart from Karen and her partner, plus an uncle, the congregation consisted of a dozen nurses and a doctor who had cared for James. Normally I might expect one or two to turn up. The presence of so many demonstrated the affection in which he was held.

Afterwards we huddled around a table in the crematorium café with tea and cakes. Tears and laughter merged as stories and memories rolled out about a man whose life had become defined by one awful moment, yet which consisted of so much more.

Travelling home afterwards, I felt blessed to have been a part of that little *ad hoc* family celebrating a man's broken life and affectionately bidding him farewell. I also wept for the family of the man James killed, doubtless still mourning his loss. Life is a complicated business.

James suffered from mental illness. Yet I have known numerous other people who committed similar crimes and worse without any apparent mitigating circumstances. And, annoyingly, some of them were probably quite decent people in other parts of their lives. I say annoyingly, because it would be much simpler if people slotted neatly into categories of 'good' or 'bad'. But they don't. We don't. Every last one of us is a moral dilemma: a maze of motives, impulses and actions, some of which we may happily own, others not so much.

John's Gospel speaks of a woman who was caught in the very act of adultery, and then dragged before Jesus by a sanctimonious crowd, baying for her blood. 'Should she be stoned to death, according to the law?' they asked. It was a trap. Whichever way Jesus responded, he was cornered. He stood for love and forgiveness; everybody knew that. But how could he flout the law without incriminating himself in the eyes of the authorities?

He paused, crouched down and wrote in the sand. Then, while the taunts continued, he straightened up and announced, 'Let any one of you who is without sin be the first to throw a stone at her.' From the woman's standpoint, it was a gamble. But Jesus knew what he was doing. The tables were instantly turned. One by one the crowd hung their heads, dropped the stones, then disappeared, until the woman was left all alone with Jesus.

'Has no one condemned you?' he asked.

'No one, sir,' she said.

'Then neither do I condemn you,' he told her. 'Go now and leave your life of sin.'*

Without a scrap of condescension, he basically said, 'Beloved woman, you are worth so much more than this.

---

* See John 8:1–11.

Go and find someone who will love and respect you, instead of using you.'

It's a marvellous story, offering one of my favourite portrayals of Jesus. Yet the question that fascinates me is this: where was the adulterous man? Why wasn't he dragged shamefully through the streets like the woman? It's impossible to catch just one person in the act of adultery. So where was he?

My very strong hunch is that he was part of the lynch mob calling for her blood. After all, none of his mates would blame him for getting caught with his loincloth around his ankles! In the twisted misogynist mind, a woman is always the baddie: the seductress leading a good man astray. It was her womanly wiles that beguiled him, obviously!

Jesus would have no part in their blokeish skulduggery. With one masterstroke he sabotaged their scheme, delivered the woman, and in the process exposed the moral ambiguity in every single one of us.

Jesus hated hypocrisy. 'First take the plank out of your own eye,' he told another crowd, 'and then you will see clearly to remove the speck from your brother's eye.'* Perhaps inspired by this, the psychologist Carl Jung

---

* Matthew 7:5.

argued that we all have a tendency to project onto others our own feelings of guilt and shame. Having buried deep in our subconscious mind things about ourselves that we dislike or disapprove of, we then go about superimposing them onto people around us. The willingness to own and embrace these 'shadow' sides to our character, Jung believed, is essential for our mental health and spiritual development.

Where does our moral ambiguity come from? Why is it that we sometimes behave like decent human beings, other times like half-witted morons? Why do we repeatedly miss the mark in being the people we aspire to be? Are we somehow inherently deranged? Or could it be that goodness and evil are connected in some deeper way in the human psyche, as Jung suggested?

Conventional Christian teaching maintains that we are not only sinners, but we are born in sin: that we have an inherent predisposition to do bad things and disobey God, and no amount of good things we do can offset this – we remain guilty in God's eyes. This is the doctrine of original sin, a teaching based on a literalistic reading of the story of Adam and Eve in the Garden of Eden.

According to Genesis, Adam and Eve dwelt in a sort of innocent paradise, living at peace with the animals and other creatures, completely unaware of their nakedness.

A single act of disobedience brought their blissful existence to an end.

God gave the couple permission to eat from any tree in the garden, apart from the Tree of the Knowledge of Good and Evil. If they ate from that tree, God said, they would surely die. However, a talking serpent told Eve, 'You will not certainly die . . . For God knows that when you eat from it your eyes will be opened, and you will be like God, knowing good and evil.'* So the couple believed this, and went ahead and ate the forbidden fruit, which led to God barring them from the Garden of Eden.

Much worse, however (for us!), according to the doctrine of original sin, Adam and Eve's 'fall' through disobedience ended up tainting the entire human race: every single one of us is infected with sin and guilt from birth. This outrageous claim has no basis in the actual story; there is no mention in the text of 'sin' or a 'fall', let alone the idea that Adam and Eve infested all their descendants. Genesis is a Hebrew text, but original sin is totally alien to Jewish thought, which maintains that sin can only ever be a matter of choice.

So where did original sin originate? Definitely not in Genesis, as we have said; but also not with Jesus, who

---

* Genesis 3:4–5.

never alludes to anything like it. Indeed, as a Jew growing up in a Jewish community, the idea would not even have entered his mind. It appears in neither the Hebrew Bible nor the New Testament, but was propagated by Augustine of Hippo in the fourth century, with a mistranslation of some words in Paul's letter to the Romans.*

Augustine believed that the original sin was Adam's sexual intercourse with Eve, the temptress. It wasn't the actual act of sex he thought was wrong, but the desire or lust Eve evoked. Sex should be a matter of the will, not desire (I don't want to imagine what this looks like in practice). Augustine's approach to original sin not only bequeathed a legacy of guilt associated with human sexuality; it also forever blighted women as sinful objects of male desire.

The plain fact is, in a scientific age the idea of original sin is gobbledegook to anyone not influenced by Christian dogma. We know that there never was a golden age from which humanity fell; we are an evolving species in an emerging universe. Adam and Eve are literary archetypes, not real people. The Garden of Eden did not exist. Nor did the tree, the forbidden fruit and the talking serpent.

---

* Augustine incorrectly translated Romans 5:12 to say that every human being was spiritually present in Adam's sin, when what Paul was actually saying was that, as a result of Adam's sin, death came into the world and we have all suffered as a result.

To read the story as a real historical event is a travesty in the twenty-first century – an insult to a beautiful text. It is a myth in the true sense of the term: a parable or wisdom tale, which may still speak deeply and truthfully to the human condition, but not factually.

No one worries whether the events in a myth – or a novel, or a film, or a poem – actually occurred. That is not the point. Myths are about meaning, not fact. They enrich rather than inform. They invite us into an imagined world, full of mysterious symbols and metaphors that may certainly cast light on human existence, but cannot describe real events or things or people.

Once we get past reading the story of Adam and Eve with strait-laced literalism, and catch the twinkle in the storyteller's eye, it begins to tell a different tale, perhaps many tales. Typical of ancient Hebrew texts, it is playful and teasing, and open to many readings.

The commandment from God not to eat from the Tree of the Knowledge of Good and Evil is magnificent satire – a joke in the very best sense. It's a set-up; of course it is. Eve will naturally eat the fruit – has God not heard of reverse psychology? The woman didn't fall; she was divinely shoved.

Seen from this perspective, eating the fruit of the Tree of the Knowledge of Good and Evil is not an act of villainy, but one of courage and liberation. Within the imaginative world of the story, had Eve not eaten the fruit human beings would have remained in a state of animal-like innocence, driven simply by ethically neutral impulses. The knowledge of good and evil is what makes us moral beings. Without that we would not be human. Genesis does not offer a tale of Paradise Lost, but Paradise Outgrown. It is not about original sin, but about the birth of conscience.*

There are a number of things I dislike about the teaching of original sin, but most of all I detest the implication that every precious child handed to me at the baptismal font is 'born in sin' and alienated from God by some inherited stain that ultimately incurs divine wrath. I just cannot believe this. Yet, tragically, it has become a basic building block in a whole psychology of guilt and shame that haunts many Christians.

I delight to baptise infants. And I do so with the passionate belief that each and every one of them is born in a state of grace – blessed by God, breathed into life by divine Spirit and loved by God unconditionally. It is grace and love that liberate and inspire us to become whole

---

* Rabbi Kushner has an excellent interpretation of the story of Adam and Eve in *How Good Do We Have To Be? A New Understanding of Guilt and Forgiveness* (Little, Brown and Company, 1996).

persons, not guilt. I therefore incite parents and godparents to take their duties seriously by nurturing the little ones in their care towards a consciousness of God's unconditional love that will never, ever let them go.

But hang on, I hear someone say: aren't children self-willed, demanding and sometimes downright naughty? And don't we all grow up into adults who screw up, and make choices that damage the lives of others and ourselves? Yes, of course. However, this is not evidence of an original sin inherited from Adam and Eve, but part of the bigger picture of how human beings have evolved over millions of years. We have become moral creatures. We have knowledge of good and evil, thank God. But we don't always make the best choices.

Post-Darwin, we now know for certain that humans never were perfect. We are mortals on a magnificent journey stretching back billions of years. We never fell from a flawless state. Rather, we have risen, through the wonder of evolution, to become moral beings with the breathtaking capacity to help shape our own destiny and that of the world in general. Behind our very best and very worst characteristics lies the immeasurable blessing of possessing the most highly evolved brain ever to exist on this planet.

Evolutionary science tells us that there is no such thing as a pre-packed human brain, a brain especially designed for Homo sapiens. As it now stands, the human brain is the result of a spectacular process of change and modification over millions of years.

> Our unique attributes evolved over a period of roughly 6 million years. They represent modifications of great ape attributes that are roughly 10 million years old, primate attributes that are roughly 55 million years old, mammalian attributes that are roughly 245 million years old, vertebrate attributes that are roughly 600 million years old, and attributes of nucleated cells that are perhaps 1,500 million years old.
>
> David Sloan Wilson*

The older parts of the brain are mainly preoccupied with survival, with things like safety, sustenance and sex. Then there are newer parts of the brain, which provide us with emotions and the desire to bond with others in nurturing relationships. More recently, we acquired the capacity to reason and rationalise, and to make choices between competing drives and instincts. Then, latterly, our brain attained self-awareness, with the ability to

---

* David Sloan Wilson, *Evolution for Everyone: How Darwin's Theory Can Change the Way We Think About Our Lives* (Bantam Dell, 2007).

explore purpose to our existence, and to experience long-ing, hope and spiritual aspiration: things that uniquely define us as human.*

Incidentally, none of this excludes God from the picture, provided we do not insist on a literal understanding of creation. Creationism is a relic from the non-scientific age. But God and evolution are not competing options. God is the Creator-Spirit: the breath in the lungs of cosmic evolution, the Ultimate Reality that transcends and fills everything. God does not 'exist', even as a super-being; that is far too small a concept. God is existence itself.

What we call 'sin', therefore, is not disobedience to a set of rules laid down by God. Sin and evil are a conse-quence of the process of evolution. So are goodness and love. Possibilities of both good and evil are built into our DNA.

The 'selfish' instincts that provide the basis of what we consider to be sinful behaviour are part of our brain structure. They are essential to the survival of our species: the will to survive even at the expense of others, the will

_____

* Michael Dowd gives a more detailed explanation of these stages of brain evolution in *Thank God for Evolution: How the Marriage of Science and Religion will Transform Your Life and Our World* (Viking, 2008).

to control territory, the will to acquire what we need, the will to have sex and reproduce.

However, this is just one part of our evolutionary legacy. We have also inherited, through later modifications, the urge to bond and nurture, to co-operate with others in pursuit of a common goal, to share resources, to care for the weak and needy among us, even to sense and address injustice. These instincts are part of our brain structure too, and enable us to make compassionate, altruistic choices that contradict our more primal survival instincts.

Primatologists like Frans De Waal have spent decades researching the behaviour of the great apes, demonstrating that alongside their sometimes violent, aggressive behaviour, apes also manifest empathy and altruism. 'Monkeys, for example, object to unfair distribution of resources, and chimpanzees do each other favours even if there is nothing in it for themselves. Bonobos are probably the most empathetic animals of all, and the genome data places them extremely close to us,' he writes.

De Waal does not describe animal goodness as morality. 'I am reluctant to call a chimpanzee a "moral being",' he says. 'There is little evidence that other animals judge the appropriateness of actions that do not directly affect themselves.' Humans, on the other hand, do make such judgements. In the symbolism of the Genesis myth, great apes have started nibbling the fruit of the Tree of the Knowledge of Good and Evil; we have eaten the whole damn thing!

De Waal's view of morality is bottom-up rather than top-down: morality isn't something imposed from the outside by God, or any other external source; it comes from within. 'It's part of our biology,' he says; 'a view supported by the many parallels found in other animals.'

He also strongly opposes what he calls 'veneer theory', an idea that has prevailed in the past among scientists and others, which sees human morality and kindness as just a thin veneer over an otherwise nasty human nature. Thomas Henry Huxley, a contemporary of Charles Darwin, championed this pessimistic vision of humanity, though Darwin himself disagreed.

Interpreting De Waal in religious terms, I would argue that morality does not amount to a codified set of behaviour dictated by a God 'out there', but is an instinctive response to 'that of God' (as the Quakers put it) within each of us.

For thirty years, De Waal has written about apes and monkeys, revealing the bottom-up roots of our human behaviours, ranging from politics to empathy, from reconciliation and justice to care for the vulnerable. Animals not only feel empathy but act upon it with displays of kindness, help and support. When we behave in these ways we are responding to instincts that have evolved in humans over millions of years.

Frans De Waal is not a religious person, but he sees no inherent conflict between religion and science. What he really opposes is narrow-minded dogmatism, both religious and non-religious: 'The enemy of science is not religion,' he states. 'Religion comes in endless shapes and forms . . . The true enemy is the substitution of thought, reflection, and curiosity with dogma.'*

In today's world, the assertion that we inherited sin from Adam and Eve makes no sense whatsoever, and there is nothing in the story in Genesis that requires us to believe it. We are a bundle of instincts, inclinations and reflexes anchored in the fathomless depths of our genetic history. In themselves, these are neither good nor bad. Everything depends on how we choose to respond to them. Clearly, people make choices in life that are imperfect, uncharitable, destructive and even downright evil. However, people also make choices that are kind, loving, sacrificial and thoroughly altruistic.

From my observation, the choices we make in life – whether to behave selfishly or unselfishly – do not

---

* Frans De Waal, *The Bonobo and the Atheist: In Search of Humanism Among the Primates* (W.W. Norton & Company, 2013).

automatically depend upon our religious beliefs or affiliations. I know utterly unselfish atheists, and completely self-absorbed Christians. Nevertheless, I continue to follow the way of Jesus because he represents, more than anyone I know, the embodiment of my highest aspirations. And in my struggling, flawed, imperfect fashion, I do my best to emulate his example. I also happily learn from the throng of others – Christians and non-Christians alike – who follow the same way.

7. I don't believe in an interventionist God

but that doesn't mean I don't believe in miracles

> *God's job is not to make sick people healthy. That's the*
> *doctor's job. God's job is to make sick people brave.*
>
> Harold S. Kushner

The death of any child is an unspeakable tragedy. But when four-month-old Jayden's teenage parents were arrested for *causing* his death, the tragedy ratcheted to a completely different level. The family's fear and confusion were exceeded only by their grief.

Ultimately, it emerged that there had been a devastating misdiagnosis of Jayden's condition. Two separate courts acquitted the couple, but not before they were further traumatised by having their other child taken from them and almost given up for adoption. I cannot even begin to imagine the hideous pain this lovely young couple went through.

But one wonderful day their little girl was restored to them. And I had the honour of burying her brother and helping the family to celebrate his tiny presence in this world. At the graveside I read an Elizabeth Jennings poem that speaks of the purity of a child's life, taken before he barely caught his breath. Jayden was not moulded by the nightmare that engulfed his parents. He never felt their pain. Not even indirectly. All he knew of this world was love and kindness; the only hands that touched him were the hands of tender care and affection. As I laid his small white box in the ground, I knew beyond doubt why I do this job.

Now, several years on, the family have slipped back into the comfort of anonymity. The ordeal is over. But when things were at their worst, and everything appeared so very bleak and terrifying, Jayden's grandmother asked me, 'Why is this happening to us? Why us?' Not only was the family grieving the death of a little boy *and* facing the possibility of his sister being permanently removed, two innocent young people were in danger of going to prison. And since all of this made headline news in the press, the family also had to deal with neighbours and others believing the young couple were possibly child-killers.

So yes, I completely understood the grandmother's question. But I had no answer. And I certainly wasn't going to cook one up. Silent solidarity is infinitely preferable to opening your mouth and proving beyond doubt that you are a well-meaning idiot. Besides, I suspect that the real question gnawing at her soul was, 'How the hell can we cope with this?' I had no answer to that either. The only thing any of us has to offer those in distress is the gift of presence. There are no answers – none worth a tinker's damn, anyway. And who needs smarty-pants advice when their entire world has fallen apart? People in pain simply need to feel the fullness of another person alongside.

I also no longer feel the compulsion to defend God when tragedies occur; though it took me years to get to this place. And given that the prevailing popular notion of God is of some kind of controlling super-being, who makes decisions about when and where to intervene in human affairs, it is not surprising that he becomes a prime target for blame when things go wrong. I don't believe in such a God, though I take care never to open up that

theological discussion with people in distress: there is a
time and place. And actually, there can be significant
therapeutic value in having somewhere to direct one's
anger. An all-powerful 'God' who seems unwilling to
intervene is a pretty convenient target.

The fact is, horrible events devoid of rhyme or reason
are everywhere in our world. And since they have no satis-
factory explanation, why are we so inclined to try to find
one? Evidently, it's part of what makes us human.
Psychologists tell us that the ability to recognise patterns
of events – and their cause – has survival value. The mind
is programmed to resist randomness; we need order,
meaning and explanation – even when none exists; *especially when none exists.*

Researchers at the University of Tennessee decided to
look into this. In one experiment they gave students
computer-generated analogies to ponder, and discovered
that unsuspecting undergraduates had little trouble coming
up with the 'logic' behind nonsensical, random phrases like
'Horse is to time as stone is to book'. However far-fetched
their interpretations, the students appeared to believe that
their explanations *were* reasonable. It's what we do: we
make sense of things, even when there is no sense.

Dr Michael Johnson, who reported the findings of this
exercise, says that the search for meaning is fundamental

to the human psyche. We can't readily settle for the inexplicable, so we use whatever means are available to us to explain randomly occurring events. If we are religious, we may see chance happenings as signs from God, or imagine them to be part of some divine master plan – the will of God. If we are just plain superstitious, we imagine that wearing our 'lucky socks' will help us to win the lottery. Frankly, I am not sure that there is very much difference between the two: superstition is often mistaken for faith; superstition *is* a form of faith, though not one that I endorse.*

So here's the thing, if you'll excuse the expression: shit happens. That's life. It happens to people all the time: good people, bad people, totally innocent people. 'Shit' is senselessly democratic in its shittiness. There is no discrimination about who deserves it and who doesn't. It is mercilessly random. And something within us rebels against this; we need an explanation.

In his Gospel, Luke describes an incident where some people told Jesus about Pilate (the Roman prefect for Judea) slaughtering a group of Galilean pilgrims who were in Jerusalem to make customary sacrifices to God. 'Look,' says Jesus, 'I know what you're thinking. But

---

* P.T. Staff, 'Shit Happens', *Psychology Today*, 1 May 1995, available at http://bit.ly/2c25Z7a.

you're wrong. This isn't God's way of punishing those Galileans for something awful they had done, for some great sin they committed. They were just regular folk like the rest: no better, no worse.'

Glancing around at the distrustful faces, he continues, 'And while we're on the subject, those eighteen people who were killed when the Tower of Siloam fell on them – they were no different to you and everyone living in Jerusalem. Shit happens! But unless you learn to see things in a different way, find a new mindset, you are walking the road of death already; you're perishing on the inside, just like the Galileans perished on the outside.'*

Jesus lived in a culture that was deeply superstitious. If something bad happened, someone had to be blamed. No doubt this is how people coped in their dangerous, uncertain world. It was a survival strategy: there had to be an explanation, a reason, so they blamed the victims, or their families, or put it down to the devil or evil spirits – they created scapegoats.

In some ways, things haven't changed. People still look for scapegoats. Some Christians still blame things on the devil and demonic spirits. In the wider society, it tends to be particular groups who are scapegoated, based on

---

* Luke 13:1–5 – a Bad Christian paraphrase.

long-standing prejudices. Isn't this a significant part of what the so-called immigrant crisis in the West is about? Someone must be blamed for the lack of decent, affordable housing, for policies of sustained austerity, for an increase in crime. So let's blame the Poles, or the Pakistanis, or anyone with different-coloured skin, or who dresses differently, or who worships in a mosque. People who are different are the 'demons' in modern society.

Naturally, there is cause and effect to some events. Certain patterns of behaviour do lead to unwelcome outcomes. But this has nothing to do with fate or karma, much less the will of God. Smoking, heavy drinking and overeating, for example, bring well-known health risks, but people do not become ill or die of such things because they are bad people or because God is punishing them or because it was 'meant to be'. There is a cause. But even then we see a random element to it: some people abuse their bodies for years and suffer badly for it; others get away scot-free. Life isn't fair.

As I write this chapter the national news contains stories of a family swept off the rocks by sudden waves on the English coast, of a young boy killed by a drunk driver as he walked on the pavement close to home, of a British-born Muslim woman having her hijab torn from her head and being called 'an immigrant bitch'. None of this is divine judgement, or because the people concerned did something wrong.

However, this does not mean that no one is to blame. It means that we need to identify who, if anyone, *is* responsible so that other tragedies, other evils, can be avoided in the future. 'Shit happens' – yes. But we must never let that be a cause of resignation or indifference. All evil can and must be resisted, every tragedy avoided wherever possible.

Most questions about religion come back to the way we picture God. Can we imagine an all-powerful, loving God who for some reason would choose to intervene in our little world while failing to respond to the crises of hundreds of thousands of innocents in other parts of the world who are starving, or thirsty, or dying unnecessarily of disease? Why would God deliver any particular people from a tragedy and leave others to be destroyed? If I believed that God could indeed relieve suffering anywhere but chooses not to, I would barrack heaven with my last breath. I would set up a change.org campaign to get countless millions of people to shame God into intervening. Actually, I would be an atheist, as an act of righteous protest.

I don't believe in divine intervention. But equally, I don't believe in divine detachment or dispassion. The first

I find incredible, the second good-for-nothing. I do in fact believe in a God who is both involved with the world and also powerfully able to transform it. But what form does divine power take? If it isn't the power to intervene – to manipulate and control worldly affairs – then how does it work?

In the minds of most people, to say that God is powerful can mean only one thing: that God is omnipotent, almighty, ultimately possessing all the power in the universe, and therefore able to do anything. This is where the problem really turns up. If God is both totally powerful and totally loving, then why are certain things allowed to happen? In order to defend God against this dilemma, we mostly fall back on the argument of free will, i.e. God has to surrender a certain amount of divine power to allow us the freedom to exercise our free will. It's an argument I myself always used to fall back on, but never, I should say, with real satisfaction or conviction. Its weakness lies in the fact that God must still remain responsible for what happens, by simple virtue of the act of choosing to permit it. If omnipotence means that ultimately God has all the power, then God cannot avoid being ultimately responsible for what transpires in the world.

And anyway, human freedom can only account for some of the causes of suffering in the world. What about natural disasters? What about the horrors inflicted by animals? What about insects that burrow into a child's eyes and cause them to be blind – the example that Stephen Fry gave when he railed at the notion of an omnipotent God in an interview on Irish TV? Fry was asked what he would say to God if he met him. He said he would tell the 'almighty': 'How dare you create a world in which there is such misery that is not our fault? It's not right. It's utterly evil. Why should I respect a capricious, mean-minded, stupid God who creates a world which is so full of injustice and pain?'*

The only 'free will' argument worth considering, in my view, is when human freedom is part of a universal principle that pervades all reality right down to atoms and beyond. It is the 'freedom' at the heart of evolution; a freedom God could not interfere with even if it were possible to do so.

Yet I fail to see why the notion of omnipotence has become fetishised into such a rigid tenet of faith. Why do we need to defend the suggestion that God is all powerful, when there are so many compelling arguments against it? Is God inevitably diminished if we set aside divine omnipotence? I don't think so. Quite the reverse. And it dismays

---

* A clip of the interview can be seen at https://www.youtube.com/watch?v=-suvkwNYSQo.

me to find good-hearted Christians contorting themselves stupid to make sense of what is 'God's plan' in patently godless circumstances, or asking, 'What is God trying to teach us through this?' The popular slogan 'God moves in mysterious ways' just sounds to me like 'I haven't got a darned clue why this is happening' – which I reckon is a more honest and healthy thing to say.

The language of divine omnipotence is, of course, drawn from the imagery of ancient monarchy, when the king's will and purpose were absolute and needed to be obeyed. In the modern world, this makes no sense. To be sure, there are still dictators who hold virtually all the power in a country, but few people will defend this as a model of good governance.

The New Testament moderates the kingly notion of God by majoring on the model of divine parenthood, which is very rare in the Hebrew Scriptures. Sadly, it is filtered through the prevailing culture of patriarchy in ancient times. A more modern, inclusive model of parenting does offer a better option than kingship to picture the divine–human relationship. The object of any right-minded parent is not to control the lives of her or his children, but to support and empower them to make their own wise and responsible choices in life, to become mature people, decent human beings who can deal effectively with what life presents. And ultimately, parents do not have the power to control what their children will do or become. Parenthood isn't about power, but about love.

The only kind of God I can personally believe in and worship is a God of love and justice: a God who would refuse to control and coerce, even if that were possible; a God who strengthens and inspires us to become all that we can be as human beings. For me, God is not a divine Superman swooping down and making everything right, or intervening magically in some circumstances but not others.

I understand God as one who suffers with the suffering, who empowers us to be strong and courageous and creative by overcoming evil and tragedy with goodness and compassion. This is the creative imagination (the Holy Spirit) in every human being, which relentlessly presses and inspires us towards a life and a world where love and justice prevail over hatred and oppression.

In the end, what I dislike most about the notion of divine intervention is that, essentially, it places God outside, and separate from, the world. I find the semantics of 'intervention' totally unhelpful and inappropriate. God does not intervene because God already *inhabits* every atom of the universe. God continuously *interacts* and *intermingles* with the laws and patterns of nature.

112

The world is 'charged' with the presence of God, as Gerard Manley Hopkins puts it in his magnificent poem 'God's Grandeur'. God is what Hopkins calls the 'dearest freshness deep down things' that dwells at the heart of everything, flaming out in sudden bursts of light and energy 'like shining from a shook foil'.*

The Swedish artist Carl Milles has a stunning sculpture entitled *The Hand of God*, which portrays a naked man standing on a huge hand, gazing into the heavens. It could mean many things, but it spoke to me of the irony of searching for a God 'out there' when God is the very ground beneath us. Perhaps the man is crying out in some desperate pain, looking for a response, without realising that the hand of God is present all along, carrying him through the suffering, bearing him up.

The God I find I can believe in is a God whose sole power is the power of love. This is the God revealed in Jesus: a God who enters the world as a helpless child, who lives in poverty, who never attempts to rise to power, who redefines authority as service, who mocks supremacy by riding into Jerusalem on an ass instead of a mighty horse, who is utterly vulnerable on a cross. For me, Christianity would be another religious system to make

---

* Gerard Manley Hopkins, 'God's Grandeur' (1877).

me yawn were it not for the theologically revolutionary story of Jesus that reveals a God whose sole existence is love itself.

Love is God's power, and love can change the world. I have no expectation of God blitzing the world with supernatural interventions. I see God's love alone as the force for transformation within events and circumstances – which is miraculous in itself.

'Miracle', however, is a loaded term. If a miracle is something that actually violates or contravenes the laws of nature, then I don't believe in miracles. That said, no one as yet has fully determined what the laws of nature are; we live in a thoroughly amazing universe whose wonders will probably never be fully understood. So I try to keep an open mind about the paranormal and the inexplicable. However, I mostly prefer to speak of the spectacular and curious powers of nature and of the human mind than of 'miracles'.

My friend Sophie's story is one of the most curious and wonderful stories that I know. In October 2014, then aged forty-eight, Sophie was diagnosed with Stage 4 'terminal cancer' and given months to live. She and her husband John have a gorgeous daughter, Gabriella, whom I was blessed to baptise four years ago when she was three. Sophie says that it is her love for her family and their love for her that literally pulls her forwards into life: 'Love is the best medicine.'

Sophie is very realistic. She knows the disease may kill her, but from the beginning of her journey with cancer she has defiantly refused to be defined by it. In the waiting room after her first dose of radiation treatment, a nurse approached and with a matter-of-fact assumption said, 'This is the date of your next appointment, Mrs Sabbage.' Sophie looked at her diary, then told the nurse she wasn't free.

'But it's your radiation appointment,' the nurse responded.

'I see that, but I'm not available,' Sophie persisted.

'Maybe I could have rescheduled whatever else I had planned,' she reflects, 'but something rose up my diseased spine that made me stand firm. I wasn't having it: I wasn't going to be told to show up, on command, without being asked if I was available.'

Desperately ill though she was, Sophie knew it was vital for her to make her own choices every step of that journey, to reschedule her treatment around her life, not the other way around, to be the author and the protagonist of her story. And what a story it has been so far. Instead of simply handing her life over to the oncologist, she decided to do her own research and make her own choices about treatments, which include conventional therapy but also incorporate a wide range of alternatives.

Sophie says that she wants to live almost more than anything. Almost. She dedicates her days, hours and minutes to extending her life 'with a fierce and unwavering' intention to raise her daughter into adulthood and grow old with her beloved husband.

'But the biggest win is not surviving cancer,' she says, 'epic as that would be. The bigger win is preserving my personhood, whatever the outcome – that hard-won "I" that neither belongs to my body nor will disintegrate with my body . . . The bigger win is knowing that I have cancer, and that cancer does not have me.'

A couple of months ago, Pat and I joined 150 people in a marquee in Kent to celebrate Sophie's fiftieth birthday – she didn't think she would see her forty-ninth. It was one of the most life-affirming evenings we have experienced. 'People, we are all terminal,' Sophie told us. 'None of us knows what the future holds.' At one stage, 150 drums were brought into the tent and we all followed a drum leader in beating out three distinct rhythms for Sophie, Gabriella and John. It was the most passionate and primal 'prayer meeting' imaginable.

Later, her oncologist announced that Sophie is rewriting the narrative of cancer – quite literally in her book

The Cancer Whisperer: How to Let Cancer Heal Your Life.* The book reverses the traditional adversarial relationship with cancer by showing how to listen to it; how to be healed by it as well as seeking its cure. Sophie isn't 'battling' with cancer, but travelling a journey towards wellness with cancer. The book is a treasure trove of jewels – practical, psychological and spiritual – that she has picked up along the way. She has also set up an online course for those affected by cancer.

I am honoured and delighted to call Sophie Sabbage my friend. She is my hero. She isn't a robot. She has days when she is overwhelmed with the sense that she may soon be gone. But she draws strength from a deeper power within her: the power of love, which has compelled her, not only to pursue the extension of her own life, but to reach out in penetrating compassion to thousands of others like her, to help show them that their life is not over, that they can take control of their situation and continue living, even in the face of death.

I have no idea what the future holds for Sophie. I hope she lives for many decades. But her life is testimony to the fact that a heart and life filled with love can transform even the most devastating circumstances, and in the

---

* Sophie Sabbage, *The Cancer Whisperer: How to Let Cancer Heal Your Life* (Hodder & Stoughton, 2015).

process extend something radically redemptive into the world.

I don't believe in an interventionist God. I believe in a God who is totally immersed in the world and in the life of humanity. I don't look to God to plunge down from the skies and make everything fine in the world, but I am convinced that there is no suffering soul whose pain God does not share.

God was in Jayden's little mind and body, sharing in his death and ushering him into a new life. God was also in the police cell, grilled with Jayden's parents and falsely accused. God lies with Sophie in yet another MRI scanner; her body is God's body, tumours and all. God lies crushed under the buildings toppled by an earthquake in Italy this week. God faces the tempest of the Mediterranean in a fragile vessel with fifty desperate refugees fleeing for safety. God's body is raped, murdered and abused in every sexual assault, every racist attack, every homophobic outrage.

God isn't a miracle cure for the ills of the world; God is the soul of the world, sharing in its pain but also breathing life and hope and courage into seemingly impossible circumstances.

8. I believe in Jesus and the three wise women

why couldn't the Son of God be a girl?

Dear God, are boys better than girls? I know you are one but try to be fair.

Sylvia*

My friend Rob Pepper (the artist who illustrated this book) was intrigued and delighted when Breast Cancer

---

* Stuart Hample and Eric Marshall, *Children's Letters to God* (Kyle Cathie, 2009).

119

Haven commissioned him to create a drawing for their Christmas concert catalogue and invitations. He was asked to:

- draw something that had a feeling of Christmas;
- create an image that wasn't clichéd, which was empowering as well as celebratory;
- make a piece that someone would want to put on their wall.

As he pondered the brief, Rob's mind travelled back to the impact breast cancer had had on his life. When he was fifteen, his mother lost her best friend Carol to the disease. It was actually this devastating event that prompted him to start painting and drawing seriously, as a way to express his anger, and a way to mourn.

Carol was a remarkable lady, Rob recalls, and her spirit lives on. 'When I think of her I'm reminded of the feelings that she seemed to embody: the spirit of recognition, love, compassion and hope.' Rob wanted his drawing to be imbued with this energy, so he chose the Epiphany (the famous Christmas story of the three 'Wise Men') because he saw these same values in that story. 'It's a moment of interfaith dialogue,' Rob says, 'and a point of recognition by the wise leaders from the East. It's also a moment of love for a newborn child. Compassion is signified by the Christ child and his symbolic hope for us all in a better future.'

Given these memories of Carol and thinking about the women connected with Breast Cancer Haven, Rob decided to draw three wise women instead of the usual trinity of men: 'Well, why not?'

The characters in the drawing are based on real-life women: Rob's wife Aimie; Jenny, a neighbour; and Apricot, who lived in London but has now returned to Portland, Oregon, with her husband and two boys. He asked these three amazing women to imagine what gift they would bring for the infant Jesus.

As a writer, Apricot said she would bring a book, which represents the wisdom of the past but also has blank pages to show that there is still much to learn and share for the future; what has already been said is still not enough.

Jenny wanted to bring an alethiometer, the golden compass from Philip Pullman's book *Northern Lights* – a fictional device that can answer hard questions – but she decided she would also bring a cake because she loves to cook for people, and she has a dream to give up her job in the afternoons and become a tea lady. 'Everyone needs a cake now and again,' Rob reflects, 'and the baby Jesus would enjoy some lemon drizzle.'

Aimie chose to bring a beautiful tree, which represents her desire to know the natural healing remedies of plants and herbs. This fitted in perfectly with the complimentary medical approach of Breast Cancer Haven.

The beauty of a good story is its capacity to be remoulded and reconceptualised for new and changing situations while still remaining true to its original meaning and purpose. Actually, in some instances, if the details of a story do not change, the story cannot remain true to its roots; meanings shift and alter in new circumstances.

I love the story of the visitation of the Magi. It's one of my favourites in the Bible. It isn't an historical event. No evidence supports that. But this doesn't make it untrue. As we have already seen, truth relates to what a story conveys, not its historicity.

Of all the four evangelists, Matthew alone records the story. Matthew was a Jew writing for a Jewish audience, putting across a theological point: Jesus is recognised by Gentiles, but not by his own people. With this story the writer dramatically depicts the birth of Christ as an interfaith event in which the fictional characters would almost certainly be Zoroastrian astrologers from Persia (modern-day Iraq and Iran).

The narrative makes no suggestion that the visitors converted to Judaism, much less to Christianity. That isn't the point. The story acknowledges that the gift of God is for all humanity, not simply one religious tradition. It also symbolises that 'gifts' from different traditions are valued and received; no single religion has it all. The Christ child is portrayed here not as the founder of a new faith (which I do not think was ever his intention) but as the symbol of something greater and grander than the whole rainbow of faiths put together: the cosmic love of God, revealed and celebrated.

Rob's picture retells the story in a completely fresh way for a fresh audience, yet the message remains the same. It's a message of hope, recognition and deep mutuality. The original story breaks down the barrier between faith traditions; the 'Women Kings' breaks through the limitations of patriarchy and masculine elitism.

Historically, women have been disempowered in society, and religion has contributed significantly to this. By asking the real-life women what gifts they would bring, and then depicting this in his drawing, Rob defends the right of women to decide what their contribution will be to religion and society, without any determination or containment by men. In principle, gender has no bearing on what a person may do, or who they may be, though society often dictates otherwise.

The problem with a story rooted in a patriarchal culture is that the patriarchal details of that story can become absolutised and control its ongoing interpretation. The backdrop to the entire Bible is a culture of patriarchy in which women are mostly disadvantaged, overlooked or demeaned. The Christian Church has still largely failed to challenge these assumptions in the text for fear of undermining the Bible's authority. We urgently need to understand and practise what theologians call 'a hermeneutics of suspicion' – a way of reading the Bible that explores and uncovers its underlying assumptions and prejudices; which asks: who is privileged by this story, by this statement or text, and who is disadvantaged?

Overwhelmingly, the Bible represents God in masculine terms: as father, or king, or lord. There are a few notable exceptions, but the dominant images of God are male. This should come as no surprise: biblical societies were male dominated, so of course God, the supreme authority, was conceived in masculine terms. But in today's world, which increasingly reaches towards gender equality, an exclusively male God is an anomaly if not an affront to many, especially when a male bias is still visibly displayed in certain attitudes and policies within the Church.

Change is occurring, but the strong perception of many people is that religion is still basically male orientated. This will continue until we see, for example, a woman

Archbishop of Canterbury, or a female Pope; more importantly, until the masculine language to describe and address God is matched by equivalent feminine vocabulary. This should not be a problem, since most of us acknowledge that divinity transcends sexual distinctions. All gendered terminology is basically a linguistic device which affirms that most people experience God in personal rather than impersonal terms. Mother, Father, Lover, Lord: none of these is literally true, yet attempts to shift towards inclusive language in prayers and liturgy still meet with solid resistance in most church communities.

But what about Jesus? How important to Christian theology is it that he was a man instead of a woman? Some years ago, a cheeky friend sent us a Christmas card that pictured a distraught shepherd running out of the stable shouting, 'It's a girl! It's a girl!' It prompted a vigorous conversation at Holy Joes the following week.

There is actually another, rather less well-known version of the joke, which tells how God *did* come as a girl, and no one took the slightest bit of notice of anything she said or did, nothing got written down or passed on, so God had to start again and send a boy. And the rest is history.*

---

* I came across this in Nicola Slee, *Seeking the Risen Christa* (SPCK, 2011).

In 1984, a bronze figure of a naked crucified woman was placed in the Cathedral of St John the Divine in New York. It caused uproar. Finding its way onto the pages of *The Times*, *Newsweek*, *Life* and other major publications, *Christa* was always going to be controversial.

The artist who created the sculpture, Edwina Sandys, granddaughter of Winston Churchill, says that women should be included in the most important image of Jesus on the cross. Bishop Walter Dennis of the Episcopal Diocese of New York disagreed. In a sermon on Maundy Thursday that year he described the symbol of a woman crucified as theologically and historically indefensible. He supported the 'women's cause' both inside and outside the Church, he said, and also affirmed that he had no problem with 'enhancing' symbols of Jesus by casting them in different colours or ethnicities, but this image went too far, 'totally changing the symbol'.

I cannot for the life of me see how a female figure on the cross totally changes the symbol. No one doubts that the historical Jesus was a man, but the artist wanted to show that women share in the sufferings of Christ too. So why should this image create such bitter opposition? Why couldn't Christ be a woman? What is the difference between this and seeing Christ as a person of colour? Unless we are seriously arguing that male is superior to female, or that God is literally a male, then the reaction can only be put down to blind, unexamined prejudice. Would it bother me if the 'Son' of God were a woman? Not in the slightest.

However, the central question for any faithful follower of Jesus does not concern his historic image, but where we may locate the figure of Christ today, *in our world*, in our socio-cultural context: who is Jesus Christ for us now? And where can we find contemporary symbols of freedom, hope and faith?

These are questions that the Filipino artist Emmanuel Garibay explores in his work. Crucial to his particular quest as a Filipino is the problem of a Christ figure that has for a long time been deeply associated with Spanish colonialism, and more recently with North American consumerism in the Philippines. How can Jesus be 'saved' from the cultural baggage we all load upon him, which is the present-day cross he is forced to bear?

The painting that introduced me to Garibay's work is called *Emmaus* and explores the intriguing story at the end of Luke's Gospel in which Jesus walks the nine miles from Jerusalem to Emmaus, and on the way meets two of his disciples, who spectacularly fail to recognise him.

On the journey, the two disciples relate the horror of what has transpired over the past few days: how their

127

master has been arrested, tried and crucified. Jesus listens with incredible restraint, then begins to discuss the Hebrew Scriptures to show them how the prophets foresaw these events. The disciples later said that it was the most enlightening, heart-warming Bible study they had ever known. Yet still they didn't realise who he was. Eventually, they arrived at Emmaus where the two compelled Jesus to stay for supper. And it was only then, as he broke the bread, poured the wine and gave thanks, that their eyes were opened to see who he really was. Then he disappeared from their sight.

It is another of my favourite New Testament stories, in which Luke brilliantly toys with the problem of over-familiarity with a particular image of Christ, and how this might domesticate his impact on our lives. He was risen now, and could never again fit into the old 'skin' in which the disciples knew him. They must let that Jesus go. That Jesus was dead and disappeared. But this new risen Jesus, this cosmic figure of Christ, was now released to meet them anywhere and everywhere. Faith is not about paying lip service to familiar images and understandings, but about being open to new and shocking possibilities.

Garibay's version of Jesus appears in the form of a woman in a red café dress, the sort perhaps worn by a woman of ill-repute, with stigmata (just in case we miss which one she is). In Filipino culture, the dress is provocative – which would be completely appropriate since Jesus often ate and drank with prostitutes and so-called 'sinners', who were counted among his friends. The disciples in the picture are laughing hilariously. They get the joke. It's on them. They had marvellously missed what was right before their eyes.

I should confess that I too fell headlong into the same 'trap' when I first saw the painting. I turned to a friend and said, 'I love this picture . . . but I still haven't worked out which one is Jesus.'

My friend smugly responded, 'Well, the woman's got holes in her hands!'

We laughed out loud, just as the figures in the picture did. And this time the joke was on me – Mr Broad-Minded Dave Tomlinson who describes himself as a feminist yet who clearly still has more blind spots than he knows.

To me, the story of Emmaus is not a record of an historical event; it's a magnificent parable. And Emmanuel Garibay's painting visually captures that parable with sheer brilliance. People are stuck with the image of a first-century man from Palestine, Garibay says. The woman in the picture is drinking and telling a joke and everybody is laughing. 'But the real joke is that people are laughing because they thought all along that Jesus was a man, and that Jesus was a Caucasian-looking guy, you know – all these conventional concepts about Jesus.'

Many conservatively minded people will see an image of three Women Kings, or of Jesus as a Filipino woman in a red dress, laughing and joking and drinking with friends, or of Christ as a naked, crucified woman, as the work of heretics: black sheep artists who need to return to the 'fold' of orthodox belief. But I reckon God is the real black sheep, the one who will not be boxed in by our stereotypical, familiar images and notions, or pinned down by rigid doctrines and creeds. God is constantly appearing where we least expect – 'Gotcha!'

I believe that so-called 'orthodox' theology of the virgin birth and fixed ideas about what it means to say that God became human have limited our perception of who Jesus Christ can be for us today, and where we might find him in our world.

For many years I have wondered why the doctrine or theory of the virgin birth is so important. I say 'theory' because no one could possibly know the intimate physical workings of Mary's womb. What difference does it make to our faith to say that Jesus was a real person with two parents? In my own case, abandoning belief in his supernatural conception has only made my faith stronger and more credible.

Much has been written in recent years about the virgin birth, and I will not add greatly to it here.* Suffice it to say that the overwhelming consensus of New Testament scholarship does not support the idea of a virgin birth, nor has it done so for a long time. And I consider it an outrage that this fact goes unacknowledged in most churches, where the average pew-sitter is never even introduced to a decent conversation about it.

To be honest, I love the Christmas story. Like everyone else, I have it embedded in my consciousness, and I still look forward to it every year with ridiculous child-like excitement. Presiding at Midnight Mass is one of my favourite priestly duties. However, I do not see why Christmas has become the most prominent of all the Christian festivals. For three centuries, the Church knew only one great feast, which was the celebration of the Christian Passover: Holy Week, Easter and Pentecost. Christ's baptism received more attention than his birth. Only in the fourth century did Christmas begin to be celebrated.

But here's the thing. We have no actual facts about the birth of Jesus, except that it did happen. The details are lost in the mists of time. Of the four Gospel writers, only

---

* I have written in more detail on the virgin birth in *Re-Enchanting Christianity* (Canterbury Press, 2008).

two – Matthew and Luke – record anything about Christ's birth. Mark and John (and Paul too) say nothing about it. They never thought it was of sufficient theological importance to mention it. Even in the accounts that we do have, the historical details are hazy and do not tally with other historical sources. But then, the Gospels were not written as biographies or actual histories of Jesus, but rather as testimonies to what the early Christian communities came to believe about him in the light of the resurrection. The Gospels are a mixture of memory, metaphor and faith – and none the worse for that.

The theme of a remarkable birth was nothing new in Israel's ancient tradition. Numerous infertile couples experienced 'miraculous' conceptions, including Abraham and Sarah who gave birth to Isaac at the utterly unbelievable age of 100, and Hannah whose delivery of the prophet Samuel is an obvious model for Luke's nativity story right down to Hannah's 'song' of celebration which closely mirrors the Magnificat, Mary's famous song. And not just in Israel but also in the wider ancient world in general, mythical stories of extraordinary births were basically a way of validating the significance or identity of an important person.

Matthew and Luke are both playing this game in their nativity narratives to underscore their belief that God was present in Jesus in a unique way. But now, in today's world, we have no need to validate a person's significance with reference to an extraordinary birth. Once anyone today seriously contemplates the biological implications of Mary being impregnated with divine sperm, it just sounds silly. And it has nothing to do with whatever we might believe about Jesus. Even Pope Benedict XVI (whom I am not accustomed to quoting), when he was a cardinal in charge of the Vatican Office for the Doctrine of Faith in 1968, wrote:

> According to the faith of the Church, the divine sonship of Jesus is not based on the circumstance that Jesus had no human father. The doctrine of Jesus' divinity would not be violated if Jesus had been the product of a normal human marriage.

I suspect one key underlying reason for the scandalous perpetuation of the supernaturalism surrounding Christ's birth is a fear that questions about it will undermine the 'simple' faith of the faithful. Repeatedly, we hear the same broken record played by conservative church leaders: that sceptical questions and 'liberal' ideas are undermining the faith. But a constant mantra about trusting the Church's historic teaching basically sounds like a pathetic attempt to shore up a creaky building which is about to tumble down.

More important to me than any of this is the question: who is Jesus Christ for us today? I am an unashamed Jesus freak: I am more inspired and invigorated by the figure of Jesus in the Gospels than by any other single human being I can name. But I am most interested in discovering where Jesus is in our world: the cosmic Christ, now liberated from the limitations of one single human body, now liberated from the restraint of being male or female, Jew or Gentile, black or white, gay or straight, now liberated from the dogma of any one religious tradition, now liberated from being merely Homo sapiens to become the creative, living presence of divine grace in the entire universe.

Everywhere I look I see the Christ figure: in a Muslim man accused of being linked with Al Qaeda who graciously invited his accuser to have tea with his family; in a busy young businessman who takes time every day to visit an elderly neighbour who has no relatives; in a teenage woman who saw a confused elderly man wandering the streets and took him to her home so help could be found; in volunteers who serve meals to the homeless; in a care home worker who invited a lonely inmate to her home for Christmas dinner with her family; in ten

134

thousand demonstrations of love and kindness every moment of every day.

The angels at the tomb of Jesus asked the women who came to anoint his body, 'Why do you look for the living among the dead?'* It's a great question. Far too much of Christianity amounts to poking around in the bones of encrusted beliefs and rituals, instead of finding the real presence of Christ in the most surprising places and forms, in the most unexpected people.

If there is one message this little black sheep would love to roar like a lion into many a church, it would be: 'YOUR CHRIST IS TOO SMALL!'

---

* Luke 24:5.

9. I believe someone who punishes his son for other people's shortcomings needs counselling

even if he is God!

The view of the cross as the sacrifice for the sins of the world is a barbarian idea based on primitive concepts of God and must be dismissed.

John Shelby Spong

Helen described herself to me as a 'church newbie'.
    She heard me talking on the radio about a Good Friday

service at St Luke's, and having felt disturbed by a recent Good Friday event at her own church she decided to email me to get my thoughts.

The service Helen had attended was a traditional three-hour vigil to recall the sufferings of Jesus on the cross. The long silence from midday to 3 p.m. is punctuated with prayers and short meditations, often based on the seven sayings of Jesus on the cross.

'I quite enjoyed the silence,' Helen wrote, 'and the meditations were good. But I was really freaked by the vicar periodically hammering six-inch nails into a large wooden cross in the centre of the church. The reverberat-ing sound of the hammering, together with a sort of mantra that it was really our (my) sins that nailed Jesus to the cross completely did my head in. I felt stifled by the overbearing sense of heaviness and guilt in the air, and by the brutality of the hammering. I've never even seen a six-inch nail before! They're massive . . . I just can't imagine what my non-Christian friends would have made of it had they walked in.'

Not all Good Friday devotions include the ritual of hammering nails into a cross, although I have been at services where it has happened. I have never inflicted it on my congregation. I'm all for a bit of drama, but hammer-ing nails into wood seems oddly literalistic, and clearly may disturb some people, especially when combined with the sort of heaviness and guilt that Helen speaks about.

There is a strain of Christian spirituality, very popular in medieval Catholicism, which fixates on the blood and gore of Christ's crucifixion. Mel Gibson brought it to a cinematographic crescendo with his grisly 2004 film *The Passion of Christ*, which I firmly intend never to watch again as long as I live.

However, it is the theology surrounding the Good Friday event that disturbs me most, especially the idea of what is known as 'substitutionary atonement'. This is the belief that Jesus had to suffer and die in our place, enduring God's wrath with human sin, in order for us to be forgiven.

The whole concept is rooted in the ancient ritual of scapegoating, where a person or animal bears the sins of others, or is unfairly blamed for their misdemeanours. Many cultures adopted some form of scapegoating ritual. Biblically, it traces back to the book of Leviticus, where a designated goat is expelled into the wilderness carrying the sins of the people. Drawing on this, the doctrine of substitutionary atonement identifies Jesus as the ultimate scapegoat for human sin, bearing the sins of the world on the cross.

Nowadays, no one in their right mind imagines that the practice of scapegoating is a good idea. It is basically seen as a psychological disorder. Even as a metaphor it is brutal and barbaric. So the concept that God (a loving, gracious and fair God, we are told) would require the painful, bloody death of anyone – let alone an innocent victim who is also his Son – in order to appease a sense of divine justice appears utterly contrary to everything we believe about the goodness, justice and love of God. I can't accept it for a moment. As others have pointed out, it ends up sounding like some kind of cosmic child abuse on God's part.

I completely understand what it is to feel the need for revenge. Daily reports of vicious crime, rape, murder, people trafficking, child exploitation and the like readily rouse in me a primal urge for revenge and violent retribution that I almost feel I could carry out myself. These are not emotions I feel proud of, however. This is not who I wish to be. I cannot see vengeance having any part in a spiritually evolved life – or in a properly civilised society.

So while in my worst moments I may indeed feel an impulse for revenge, my better self repudiates that and awakens me to a more imaginative, non-violent, hopefully grown-up response. Violence cannot possibly be a decent or useful way to respond to evil in the world. For this reason, I can't for the life of me believe in (much less admire or worship) a God whose anger is quelled by violence and blood sacrifice. How could I revere a God with less virtue, less humanity, than I myself aspire to?

Is this wishy-washy liberalism? Not unless you consider Jesus to be a wishy-washy liberal. Throughout his life he totally disavowed violence and revenge. He taught us to love our enemies and pray for those who persecute us. He said that if anyone strikes you on the right cheek, turn the other also. He even forgave his tormenters as they nailed him to the cross. Seen through the lens of Jesus in the Gospels, any God that required the spilling of blood to satisfy justice would be sub-Christian, to say the least.

Jesus was arrested by the guards of the Sanhedrin, a ruling body in Jerusalem, and executed by the Romans. He was crucified: the Roman equivalent of being hanged, injected with a lethal substance, gassed or placed before a firing squad – but less humane. The comedian Lenny Bruce said that if Jesus had been killed twenty years ago, Catholic schoolchildren would be wearing little electric chairs around their necks instead of crosses.

But why was Jesus killed? Well, to start with, the authorities despised him. To them, he was a troublemaker, an agitator. The Israelite establishment was in a delicate position at the time. They had their own semi-independent king but were nevertheless clearly under the rule of Rome, so it was vital to keep things sweet with the Roman occupiers. This meant maintaining control of their own population, keeping them compliant. They didn't see Jesus as particularly helpful in this regard. He denounced temple corruption, spoke out against injustice and generally stirred things up. He had no obvious political aspirations and posed no direct threat, but he was a pain in the rulers' rear end.

Chiefly, Jesus gave downtrodden people hope that things could be different. He proclaimed a new order, a new dimension called the kingdom of God – which basically posed the question: what would the world be like if God were king instead of Caesar? This empowered people to stand taller, to find greater self-worth, to live more fully, more purposefully. And this was not good news to authorities who wanted to keep people under control.

Jesus was an outsider to the ruling classes. He had no formal training or recognised position; he wasn't a priest or a civic functionary. He was a mystic, a healer and a charismatic preacher who upended the religious and social culture of the day by giving dignity to women, children and Gentiles, and by eating and drinking with marginalised folk like publicans, prostitutes and other ne'er-do-wells. Worse still, he told the religious leaders that this rag-tag bunch of 'sinners' was entering the kingdom of God ahead of them. He was the people's 'working-class hero', who used his wit and wisdom to give the authorities a bloody nose.

Probably the final straw in his catalogue of aggravating offences came when Jesus entered the temple and overturned the tables of the moneychangers and traders, who were legendary for ripping off the poor, but approved by the temple authorities, who got a healthy cut of the takings. Jesus screwed with the state of things. For this reason the religious leaders dragged him before Pilate, the Roman prefect, on trumped-up charges to have him killed.

Most Christians claim that there is more to it than this: that Jesus didn't simply die at the whim of the authorities, but that his death was part of God's bigger plan to save the world. It's a theme embedded in countless hymns, sermons, songs, films and novels: Jesus died for our sins. But what does that mean? How could his death save us from our sins?

In a nutshell, the most common answer to this question goes a bit like this:

- We are all born sinners, because of the disobedience of our primitive ancestors, Adam and Eve, who ate the forbidden fruit in the Garden of Eden.

143

- Because of this, our relationship to God is irreparably broken. No amount of good we do in this life can fix it, or rectify our sinful state. In and of ourselves, we are a lost cause.

- The good news, however, is that God sent Jesus, who took upon himself our sin when he died on the cross. God punished him instead of us, so now we can be forgiven and reconciled to God, *provided* we put our trust in what Jesus did and accept God's gift of salvation.

- If we do this, we will be able to go to heaven when we die, and live with God for ever. Otherwise . . . don't even ask!

The moral and practical problems with this scapegoating theory of atonement are endless, not least because it seems to suggest some kind of jiggery-pokery transaction within God's own head. As New Testament scholar Walter Wink asks, what is wrong with this God 'whose legal ledgers can be balanced only by means of the death of an innocent victim'?* Why is a sacrificial scapegoat necessary to make forgiveness possible? How could it even help? And how are we to make sense of a

---

* Walter Wink, *The Powers that Be: Theology for a New Millennium* (Doubleday, 1998), p. 87.

schizophrenic deity who all of a sudden changes his attitude towards people when another person dies in their
place?

Little wonder that so many people turn their back on
such a monstrous and illogical notion of God. As Walter
Wink declares, 'Against such an image of God the revolt
of atheism is an act of pure religion.'*

Have a think about this: Jesus actually went about
forgiving people all the time. No one had apparently told
him that he would need to die before he could do that! He
also taught others to forgive freely. On one occasion,
when Peter thought he was being generous by offering to
forgive a person seven times, Jesus told him, 'Try seventy-
seven times!' – which is just another way to say, 'Stop
counting!'

But even before Jesus appeared, the Hebrew Scriptures
are packed with images and references to a merciful,
forgiving God who required no sacrifices. There are even
places in the Bible where the prophets announce that
God is sick and tired of offerings and blood sacrifices
and make it clear that action is what is required: 'Cease
to do evil,' they suggest. 'Learn to do good; seek justice,
rescue the oppressed, defend the orphan, plead for the

---

* Walter Wink, *Engaging the Powers* (Augsburg Fortress, 1992),
p. 149.

widow.' In other words, 'Don't come begging for forgiveness (that is not the issue); just start doing the right thing!'

Forgiveness is not easy. We all know that. But people forgive all the time, even when the price of it seems impossibly high. I recently stumbled on 'The Forgiveness Project', an amazing undertaking set up by a freelance journalist called Marina Cantacuzino. Having reported on lots of wonderful and challenging stories about forgiveness, she decided to give an online platform for people to share their own stories and struggles.

'The Forgiveness Project' website offers heaps of accounts of amazing people who have suffered diabolical atrocities yet have learned to absolve their oppressors: people like Jude, whose mother was killed by a terrorist bomb in Northern Ireland; Madeleine, who was violently raped and tortured when she was thirteen; Wilma, whose young teenage daughter was abducted and murdered; and Dave, who was mercilessly abused by his mother and brother and ended up scarred for life. Each of these people discovered the way of forgiveness. I read their stories, and many more besides, weeping, not simply because their stories were painful, but in gratitude for the courage and fortitude

146

of people who have walked the path of forgiveness so magnificently.*

Over the years I have sat with more people than I could ever count who have sustained the direst of injuries, physically and emotionally, yet who have gone on to pardon their tormentors. The capability of human beings to forgive, even when there are no obvious signs of remorse or regret, staggers and humbles me, but also leaves me flabbergasted by the idea that God, the source of our deepest and truest humanity, could not also forgive without requiring some form of payback.

The God I believe in, the God of Jesus Christ, forgives unilaterally. Nothing is required: no shedding of blood, no flagellation, no sacrifices or penance. God forgives freely because that is the divine nature. And just in case anyone doubts what I am saying, Jesus underscores the point with his stunning, subversive parable of the prodigal son, which stands as a blistering critique of the concept of a God who needs some kind of blood sacrifice to atone for sin.

As the writer Bob Seidensticker ironically points out, 'If we were to twist the Prodigal Son parable to match the crucifixion story, the father might demand that the

---

* See http://theforgivenessproject.com.

innocent son be flogged to pay for the crime of the prodigal son. Where's the logic in that?"*

The cross of Jesus has a political meaning. He was crucified by the Romans. Crucifixion was a Roman form of execution (had the Jews killed him, he would likely have been stoned or beheaded). And under Roman law three types of offenders were crucified: pirates, rebellious slaves and enemies of the state. Jesus clearly wasn't a pirate or a rebellious slave, so why was Pilate persuaded that he was an enemy of the state? Why would a peasant healer who preached love of one's enemies be seen as a threat to the mighty Roman Empire?

The problem was, he did more than heal people and preach love. Jesus also preached justice – not Rome's justice, but God's. The Jesus scholar John Dominic Crossan argues that Pilate got it right: Jesus was a subversive – much more than Pilate could have imagined. Preaching compassion can get you canonised. Preaching justice will more likely get you crucified. Jesus really did challenge Rome's authority, not by leading an insurgency in any conventional sense, but by proclaiming the kingdom of God, a different kind of rule based on

* Bob Seidensticker (23 November 2011), available at https://www.patheos.com/blogs/crossexamined/2011/11/atheism-jesus-crucifixion-story-does-god-exist.

forgiveness, love and justice; and that was the greatest challenge of all.

In the cross of Jesus we see the ultimate expression of divine grace: whatever we do, however vicious, stupid or malicious, God will never stop loving us. The suffering of Jesus is a sacrament of divine love: a powerful means of transforming our lives and the life of the world – not because it pays a debt to God, but because it opens up a different way to be. By absorbing all the violence, personal evil and systematic injustice of the world in the death of Jesus, God invites the world to be saved from itself. Jesus didn't come to change God's mind about us, but to change the way we see and understand God; more importantly, to change the way we respond to God.

However, it is not just by his death that Jesus saves the world, but by the whole Jesus-event, from birth, through life and ministry (with its proclamation of the good news of God's kingdom), death and resurrection. The message of the Jesus-event can be summed up in this statement: 'I came that they may have life, and have it abundantly.'* Everything about Jesus was directed at calling people to come alive, to be fully awake to all that life could be in the purpose of God. Being 'saved' in Jesus' terms wasn't

---

* John 10:10 NRSV.

about going to heaven when you die, but about experiencing an abundant life now.

Apparently, in the original Aramaic that Jesus and his followers used, there is no word for 'salvation'. Salvation was understood as a bestowal of life; to be saved was 'to be made alive', or to be fully alive. For the earliest Christians, therefore, Jesus was not the Saviour (as we have come to think of that) but the 'Life-giver'.*

Throughout the Gospels, Jesus never speaks of 'receiving' salvation; he called people to follow him, to be part of his way and therefore come alive. In more contemporary language, Jesus liberated (saved) people from enslavement to ego, the drug of self-importance, and invited them to discover the path of vulnerability, love, generosity and service. The cross speaks of this more than anything else: the abandonment of ego, winning by losing, love given without measure. Indeed, the whole Jesus-event imagines a God separated from self-asserting power, a God whose only existence is love. This is the path Jesus invited his followers to enter, the path of salvation.

The path begins with repentance, a word now wrongly enmeshed in associations of guilt and shame. But the

---

* For more on this, see Cynthia Bourgeault, *The Wisdom of Jesus: Transforming Heart and Mind – A New Perspective on Christ and His Message* (Shambhala, 2008).

Greek word *metanoia* actually means a change of mind, a new mindset. To repent is to open up to a new consciousness: about ourselves, about other people, about the world – about God. Yes, this will include turning away from practices and thought patterns that are selfish or damaging and driven by ego alone, but essentially, to repent is to come alive; to discover a new wholeness; to begin to evolve spiritually; to be saved.

I believe that the mystery of the whole Jesus-event (his birth, life, teaching, death and resurrection) offers salvation, by showing us what a 'saved' life looks like, and by inviting us to be part of this way: to live as passionately as Jesus lived, to love as extravagantly as he loved, and like him to become all that we can be as whole human beings.

10. I believe the 'empty tomb' is a distraction
what Easter faith really means to me

The proof that God raised Jesus from the dead is not the empty tomb, but the full hearts of his transformed disciples.

Clarence Jordan

It was a Monday evening in the upstairs room of a north London pub, and I had been invited to give a talk to a packed audience of 'Christians and sceptics' on the subject 'How to Reinvent God'. The genial host quipped that I might come under fire from both sides: the Christians and the atheists. I joked that I would stand close to the door – just in case!

In the event, I had a fun evening that finally came to an end when the bar closed. And there was no 'fire' from either side – though I probably went down better with the atheists than the Christians.

During the Q&A after the talk, one man impressively listed what he detected were some of my theological influences. He then went on to ask where I stood on the resurrection of Jesus. 'St Paul states that belief in the physical resurrection is the one basic essential to being a Christian,' he said. 'Do you believe in the resurrection? And if not, can you rightly describe yourself as a Christian?'

'It really depends what you mean by physical resurrection,' I responded. 'If you mean, was the body of Jesus resuscitated, or literally restored to life, then I don't believe that. But incidentally, I don't think Paul believed that either.' (From the corner of my eye, I saw a woman shaking her head in silent disapproval.)

The line of questioning is familiar to me. I face it all the time, especially when addressing certain kinds of Christian audiences. And I understand why: the resurrection is indeed a cornerstone of Christian faith. Without the Easter story there would be no Christianity.

What is debatable, however, is what the Easter experience really was: what actually happened. Here a gulf opens up between those whose faith hinges on a body being literally restored to life, and others like me who insist that resurrection means something more than (and different from) physical resuscitation.

For those who interpret the resurrection in literal terms, the issue is very straightforward. Jesus was crucified on Good Friday. His dead body was laid in a tomb, where it remained for three days. Then on Easter morning, through a mighty act, God restored his body to life and Jesus walked out of the empty tomb. He continued on Earth for a further forty days, making various appearances to his disciples, and then finally ascended into heaven. There can be no compromise on this, many people claim. If the body of Jesus was not physically restored to life, then Easter is a sham. And any departure from this belief is a departure from the true faith.

Well, if that really is all there is to say on the matter, then I need to join the hordes of modern-day people who have given up on Christian belief. Yet I haven't given up on it, because there is plenty more to say.

I have absolutely no doubt that something utterly extraordinary happened to the disciples after the death of Jesus that convinced them he had conquered the boundary of human death, and that he remained a living presence in their midst. However, the accounts in the Gospels of how this came about are far from straightforward. They are, in fact, confusing, ambiguous and, in places, downright contradictory. This doesn't mean that the writers were lying, or deceiving their readers. It simply highlights the fact that the Gospels were never written as history or biography as we understand those terms. They are testimonies – a mixture of memory, metaphor and faith – to a phenomenon that utterly transformed their lives, and gave birth to the Church.

However, for many people today, the greater problem with a literalist understanding of Christ's resurrection is that we live in the twenty-first century – an age fashioned and shaped by the development of science and critical reason, which must also now be taken into account. It is no longer possible to believe something simply because the Church says it is true, or because it is in the Bible. We must also think for ourselves, question what we hear, use our God-given intelligence. This doesn't mean that science is always right, or that Scripture is excluded from the picture, but for faith to be remotely viable for most people today, it must exist in open dialogue with reason. Christian tradition is not simply a set of texts, creeds and doctrines to be unquestioningly believed, but an evolving conversation between past and present: between a faith handed down, and a faith being reborn in a new situation.

Having grown up with a naive acceptance of what the Church taught me about the resurrection, I finally reached a point, over thirty years ago, when the accumulated doubts and questions shoved to the back of my mind refused to keep silent any more. So I sat down one day to let them speak. Could I really believe that a decomposing corpse revived after three days then walked out of the tomb? Was that what I was supposed to believe? I really didn't think I could. Not any longer. So I went on a search to find out what I could believe.

First, I contemplated the more rational explanations people come up with. Perhaps Jesus wasn't really dead when they buried him; maybe he was in a state of deep unconsciousness from which he recovered in the cool atmosphere of the tomb. Was his body taken by the Romans and disposed of elsewhere? Historians tell us that prisoners were generally buried by the Romans and not by friends or relatives, so could his remains have been dug up from a shallow grave by hungry animals and consumed? Was his resurrection an apparition or trance brought on by an altered state of consciousness in the disciples? Or, since the Gospels were written long after the event, were the resurrection accounts created by Christians to validate their belief in Jesus?

I didn't particularly buy into these more rational explanations, any more than I felt I could now live with a simplistic belief in the resuscitation of his body. After all, how could anyone know? It just felt like a mountain of pointless speculation. Nothing was provable. Much more importantly, however, none of it seemed at all consequential to my life or faith, to my daily attempts to follow Christ's way. Jesus remained a living reality in my experience whatever I believed.

Now, all these years later, I have long since given up worrying about what actually happened on a Sunday morning two thousand years ago. Arguments about the 'empty tomb' leave me cold as the grave. Yes, something extraordinary did happen, but what does it all mean for me today, for the world and its problems?

Clarence Jordan, a farmer and New Testament Greek scholar, said that 'the proof God raised Jesus from the dead is not an empty tomb, but the *full hearts of his transformed disciples*. The crowning evidence that he lives is not a vacant grave, but a *spirit-filled fellowship*.'

Clarence was born in Georgia in 1912, the seventh of ten children in a Southern Baptist family. In church he learned a vision of racial equality, singing the children's chorus:

> Red and yellow, black and white,
> All are precious in God's sight . . .

But as he grew older, he became disturbed by the reality of racial discrimination that he witnessed all around – including in the segregation at church on Sunday mornings – which did not match the lyrics of the song.

After graduating from high school, he earned a degree in agriculture, then a PhD in New Testament Greek. Of all he read, Jesus' Sermon on the Mount gripped Clarence, and led him to found a community called Koinonia Farms, named after the Greek word for 'fellowship'. He decided to bring together his twin passions for agriculture and Scripture with a radical commitment to follow the way of Jesus.

Clarence, his wife and another couple bought 440 acres of land south of Atlanta to turn his vision into reality. Straightaway it caused trouble because of the way he put racial equality into practice, inviting the workers to eat together regardless of race. The Ku Klux Klan leapt into action, and there were many ugly clashes with local racists. One of Clarence's favourite challenges to the racists was: 'Your choice seems quite clear. It is whether you will follow your granddaddy or Jesus Christ.'

Eventually, Koinonia Farms gave birth to Habitat for Humanity International, under the leadership of Millard Fuller, a supporter of Clarence's radical ideas. This is an international charity devoted to building 'cheap, decent, and affordable' housing, a 'Christian housing ministry', which addresses issues of poverty all over the world. Its mission statement is: 'Seeking to put God's love into action, Habitat for Humanity brings people together to build homes, communities and hope.'

Clarence Jordan believed passionately in the living reality of Jesus Christ in the world. However, the proof of Christ's resurrection lay not in an empty tomb or a gravestone rolled away, but in lives aflame with the Spirit of Christ. For him, crucifixion and resurrection were not simply events in the past, but continuing realities.

In a similar vein, at St Luke's we approach Good Friday not simply as a reminder of the historical crucifixion, but as a way of responding to the sufferings of Christ in the world today. Each year we invite members of our community to create 'stations' – pictures, images and installations – that depict or symbolise the suffering of Christ in present-day people and situations, and these become a focus in our Good Friday service.

Last year our theme was 'Christ of the Displaced'. Through the long days of Lent we centred our thoughts and prayers on the many forms of displacement in the world: homeless people on our own streets in London, people escaping domestic violence, refugees and asylum seekers fleeing war zones and places of extreme poverty. In one of my talks I showed a picture of Jean François Millet's dark and startling depiction of *The Flight into Egypt*, when Mary and Joseph fled with their young child from Herod's brutal slaughter of the children. We also pondered Timothy Schmalz's amazing sculpture of a homeless Jesus lying on a park bench under a blanket.

Among the twenty or so 'stations' arrayed around the church on Good Friday was a magnificent icon of Christ holding a small Syrian child in a life jacket at the edge of the Mediterranean, created by nineteen-year-old Daisy. Sheena painted fourteen mini Stations of the Cross based on people in the 'Jungle' refugee camp in Calais, and added an additional picture on Easter morning to represent the resurrection. Janek hung a large cross, covered with a map of the world, highlighting places of painful displacement. And above the round altar in the centre of the church, Hilary suspended a huge crown of thorns made from razor wire on which small patches of gold denoted the presence of Christ in the suffering of those who are confined or excluded. There was also a beautiful but shocking image created by Laura of Noddy, the character from Enid Blyton's children's books, crucified, which forcefully conveyed the loss of innocence in children caught up in conflict, upheaval and dislocation.

It isn't our intention to set aside or disrespect the sufferings of Jesus on the cross two thousand years ago, yet the real scandal of Good Friday is when we overlook the suffering of Christ that surrounds us every day. Without responding to this in some way, our contemplation of the historic crucifixion may amount to little more than religious sentiment.

How are we to bring life and hope to people living under the shadow of death in our world? This is the real challenge within the death and resurrection of Jesus.

Resurrection is not simply about the hope of life beyond death, but about the capacity to envisage and embody resurrection life in the here and now: to bring life and hope into situations of death and despair, to shine light and wisdom into darkness and fear, to overcome oppression and injustice with acts of liberation and compassion. We need to imagine ways to turn 'resurrection' into a verb instead of a noun, to treat it as a quality of life rather than an event in the past, or the future. This isn't to deny or degrade the reality of resurrection as a past event or a future hope, but to stress the limited usefulness of speculation, and the priority of living in the now.

Few people in my lifetime have practised resurrection more powerfully than Desmond Tutu. Having grown up under the hatred, bigotry and brutality of apartheid, he refused ever to believe in its inevitable victory. He lived and worked as if apartheid's days were numbered, even when it appeared invincible. And when it was finally toppled, he knew that hatred would not be overcome with more hatred, so he laboured towards a new state of things with the South African Truth and Reconciliation Commission. We began our Easter morning service last year with a sung version of Desmond Tutu's famous prayer, which I see as a resurrection creed:

> Victory is ours
> Goodness is stronger than evil;
> Love is stronger than hate;
> Light is stronger than darkness;
> Life is stronger than death;
> Victory is ours through him who loves us.*

---

* From Desmond Tutu, *An African Prayer Book* (Doubleday, 1995).

In my Easter Day sermon, I pointed to other accounts of people practising resurrection, especially in the context of the refugee crisis. One story I discovered on the Red Cross website told of Beshwar, a twenty-five-year-old man from a village near Mosul, who fled with his family from the conflict in Iraq, looking to find a new life in Britain.* Beshwar plays seven instruments, speaks excellent English and expends great energy trying to help others. Along with 3,000 other refugees, mostly Syrian and Iraqi Kurds, including 300 children, he found himself in the Grand-Synthe camp near Dunkirk.

'The only thing we have here is hope,' he says. 'There's no clean water, no showers; there aren't even enough toilets. But what else do we have?' The inhabitants spend their days trying to keep warm and dry. 'On one side I am happy because I can help my people here. We share the sadness,' Beshwar says. 'But I never dreamt I would be living somewhere like this.'

The language used to portray refugees and migrants is often unsavoury and dehumanising. But 'spend any time in the company of the people', an aid worker points out, 'and you soon discover that they have big hearts and are incredibly hospitable'.

---

* See blogs.redcross.org.uk/emergencies/2016/02/meet-mother-jungle-dunkirk-refugee-camp/ (10 February 2016).

In a makeshift hut, which is missing two walls, Beshwar's mother Roonak stands over a steaming pot of stew on a stove fuelled by coal and wood. 'Kurdish bean stew,' she says, smiling, before reeling off the ingredients. There's a small crowd of people around the hut, eager for a serving.

'I cook for everyone because all the Kurdish people are my family. There's nowhere else to cook, so we have to help each other,' Roonak says. 'It's hard in the camp. There's nowhere to wash and it's so cold at night. I never thought I would be living somewhere like this. But in a way I feel safe here. There are no guns, no bloodshed.'

'We are not uneducated. We have morals,' she continues. 'It is not about this muddy place or these dirty clothes that we wear. Under these clothes are flesh and bones. We are all the same. We hate the label "refugee". We are people. But we are refugees because of war. We want peace, we want to find a place to live.'

People like Beshwar and Roonak (and there are plenty of them on the long and hazardous refugee and migrant trail across the Mediterranean and through Europe) shine as beacons of resurrection life and hope in the midst of death and despair. They are living proof that goodness is stronger than evil, love is stronger than hate.

We cannot all be Clarence Jordans or Desmond Tutus, and thank goodness most of us do not find ourselves in the dreadful predicament of people like Roonak and Beshwar, yet we must commit ourselves to being part of a movement of resurrection in our world instead of standing around while Christ is crucified afresh in countless innocent victims.

I am not interested in speculative questions about what did or did not happen to the body of Jesus two thousand years ago; arguments about the empty tomb do nothing for me. What I am deeply interested in, however, is the question: how can we incarnate the living presence of Jesus Christ in our lives, in our world today? How can we breathe resurrection life into situations of misery and devastation? This is what Easter means to me.

That said, there is one other significant dimension to flag up. As well as being a call to action, Easter is also an invitation into mystery. My rational mind cannot accept a literal interpretation of the resurrection – a corpse returning to life – but what rationalism very easily overlooks or neglects is that there are things in the universe that cannot be encompassed by reason. Truth is more than fact, and not all truth can be categorised as either fact or fiction.

'Mystery' is sometimes used as an intellectual cop-out, but any intellect that does not sometimes stand in awe and wonder before that which is incomprehensible is as good as dead. As I said earlier, I have no doubt that something extraordinary occurred to the disciples which convinced them that the death of Jesus was not the end; that in some mysterious way he remained a living presence in their midst. And millions of others since, myself included, testify to something similar.

Probably my favourite Christian ritual is the Easter Vigil at St Luke's, through which I re-enter the mystery of resurrection each year.

The service begins at 11.15 p.m. on the Eve of Easter. The congregation are seated in a darkened church, lit only by seven large candles. The chairs are arranged in concentric circles, punctuated by six candlesticks. In the centre is a small table on which stands the previous year's paschal candle (a large candle that is renewed every Easter, signifying Christ's presence in the church). The first part of the service consists of six readings retelling the story of God's love for the world. After each reading, a candle is extinguished. Eventually, at about 11.45 p.m., in the deep gloom, the choir sing the old African-American spiritual 'Were You There When They Crucified My Lord?' After that, the final candle is taken from the room, and we sit in silent darkness for about ten minutes, invited to sense the stillness of Christ's tomb.

On the stroke of midnight, as the church bell heralds the arrival of Easter, an intense flash sears the darkness, and great light bursts through the east window (from a large theatrical lamp in the vicarage garden), filling the chancel area; a new paschal candle is lit, and the proclamation fills the church:

> The light of Christ! *Christos anesti!* Christ is risen!
> The light of Christ! *Christos anesti!* Christ is risen!
> The light of Christ! *Christos anesti!* Christ is risen!

The congregation then process into the chancel, stand around the altar and celebrate the first mass of Easter, while the choir sing the *Exultet*, an ancient hymn of praise for the Easter Vigil.

The whole thing sends shudders down my spine, and each time I know afresh that resurrection is a mysterious reality totally different from the mere resuscitation of a crucified body.

An Easter Note to Self
- Look beyond the darkness of present circumstances, and lean towards the light; never let gloomy times define who you are.
- Ask questions and doubt fearlessly, but never forget that life is a mystery.

- Remind yourself often that doing what you know to be the right thing is a way of winning even when you lose.
- Bring hope and laughter into places of tears and despair, but never try to give 'answers' when you don't have them.
- Actively oppose prejudice, discrimination and oppression wherever you see it, even when it makes you unpopular.
- Care for the Earth and its creatures, and live in the best possible way that all may flourish.
- Where there is conflict, do everything you can to spread peace and reconciliation; and learn to apologise as naturally as breathing.

11. I believe truth is stranger than fact

was Jesus really an astronaut?

Myths are heroic struggles to comprehend truth in the world.

Ansel Adams

When Nicholas and Verity Mosley moved to a house in Holloway, just across the road from St Luke's Church, their friends thought they were mad. They said, 'You won't have any friends there; you're miles away from any of us.' To which Nicholas replied (with a twinkle in

171

the eye), 'Well, my father was in Holloway for four years.'

By 'Holloway', Nicholas was referring to the nearby prison, where his father, the infamous Oswald Mosley, founder of The British Union of Fascists, was interned during the Second World War along with his wife Diana Mitford. Their fascist politics and friendship with members of Hitler's inner circle were considered dangerous. However, that was a long time ago, and had nothing to do with Nicholas, who publicly derided his father's outlook.

It was Verity who first wandered into the church one day when there was no service going on. 'It's the most extraordinary place,' she told Nicholas. 'All the furniture has been taken out!' On the following Sunday, she came to a service.

'You must come along,' she said.

Nicholas wasn't so sure.

'I thought it was going to be "happy-clappy",' he recalls, 'but the music was wonderful.'

So the couple started attending regularly, and became very dear friends to me and Pat.

Nicholas describes himself as a storyteller. That's a bit of an understatement: he is a Whitbread Award-winning author of over thirty books, some of which have also been turned into films.

Nicholas says that when people ask him how he can believe in Christianity, the idea of God becoming human, he tells them, 'I can believe it because it's such a good story. God as a baby? It's such a good story that it has lasted for two thousand years. It's either completely incomprehensible, or else it is the thing we call T.R.U.E. I don't know whether things happened exactly like that but to me this is such a good story that it must be true.'

The question as to what 'true' really means has exercised Nicholas for much of his adult life. His autobiography *Efforts at Truth** (a turn of phrase I have borrowed several times in this book because I find it so evocative) begins with the age-old debate about which form of writing can tell more of 'truth': fiction or non-fiction. Unsurprisingly, I think, Nicholas concludes that each can speak truth in its own way. But he argues that we get closer to the real truth when there is an interplay between the two, which is what his autobiography attempts to achieve.

Nicholas defends his Christian faith, not with dogma or arguments, but with the gleeful embrace of a story: 'God as a baby? It's such a good story that it must be true.' He isn't bothered about facts, or whether it happened exactly like that; it's a good story and that is

---

* Nicholas Mosley, *Efforts at Truth* (Minerva, 2011).

enough. Truth for the novelist isn't about fact, but something grander and more encompassing.

For many people, of course, this won't do. In their eyes, truth must of necessity be based in fact. And oddly enough, this is something that black and white fundamentalist Christians and black and white atheists share in common. The one says that if the story isn't factual it *cannot* be true; the other says it cannot be true *because* it isn't factual. These are flipsides of the same assumption. Both are wrong. Of course, a story can absolutely be true in the deepest and fullest sense without being factual. Anyone who loves art or poetry or novels or music knows this. Facts are important, for sure, and they have their place, but too often they leave us on the surface of an event or subject, while art – even when it has little connection with fact – can take us right beneath the surface.

The Bible is full of stories and myths that modern scholarship determines probably did not actually occur, or which make no sense today if taken as they stand. But this does not mean that they are untrue. Indeed, they may be T.R.U.E. as Nicholas likes to put it.

It is often assumed that myths are the opposite of history or science. But in fact, they simply have a different role: one of interpreting the meaning and significance of life, rather than simply examining facts and data. Myths are not lies or untruths. They are imaginative devices, usually in narrative form, to make sense of the world. They shape our perception of things.

Traditional peoples always conveyed their most important beliefs and values through stories, or through symbols and rituals. And myths haven't gone away. Humans are meaning-making creatures, and we still explore meaning best with stories – whether through novels, or theatre, or films, or TV. There is a good reason why people sometimes confuse the storyline in a soap opera with reality, or why we are so moved by a film even when we know that it is a fiction. Stories are the most basic way in which we perceive the world, constantly crossing the line between the thing we are watching or reading and our own lived reality. As the writer Philip Pullman says, 'After nourishment, shelter and companionship, stories are the thing we need most in the world.'

Nowadays there is also a whole strand of Christian theology known as 'narrative theology', which focuses on the revelation of God through stories rather than abstract ideas and concepts. Jesus himself chose storytelling as his favourite kind of theology. And it is his stories that we mostly remember. The parable of the good Samaritan, for example, communicates far more effectively than any sermon or theological idea the importance of caring for strangers. The very term 'Samaritan' has become synonymous with doing good for others – which is ironic, considering Samaritans were hated by Jews at the time. And the scandalously unconditional devotion of the father figure in the parable of the prodigal son communicates the nature of grace, or God's unconditional love, infinitely more evocatively than any piece of theological dogma.

But I would go further, to suggest that some of the stories about Jesus in the Gospels are also parables – and none the worse for that. Take, for example, the story of the risen Jesus walking and talking with two of his followers on the road to Emmaus. As Luke tells the story, the two dejected disciples were walking home to Emmaus following the crucifixion. As they churned over what had happened, a stranger approached and joined the conversation. He went on to interpret the crucifixion eloquently in the light of the Hebrew Scriptures. Yet even though they were moved and fascinated by his words – the same Jesus they had listened to dozens of times – they failed to recognise him. When they reached Emmaus the disciples prevailed on the stranger to join them for supper. Still they did not recognise him, until he broke the bread at the table and their eyes were opened.

Am I really supposed to believe that this happened as it is described? Do I have to believe that two people actually walked for miles with someone they knew very well, talking about him and discussing what had happened to him, without even recognising who he was? And what difference does it make if I don't believe it? The point is, it is a great story, a truthful story that reminds me again and again to expect Jesus to turn up anywhere, especially in the form of a stranger. Actually, I suspect Luke's real intention was to affirm the presence of Christ in the Eucharist – and at every meal. It's an archetypal story. As John Dominic Crossan states, 'Emmaus never happened. Emmaus always happens.'*

Some stories in the Bible, if read literally, become ridiculous, but this does not stop them from being T.R.U.E. The story of the ascension of Jesus into heaven is an excellent example. Taken at face value it is absurd, almost comic: a man floating away to heaven on a cloud as if on a magic carpet, or hovering in the air like Mary Poppins with her brolly. How high did he go? Where did he stop? If he made it into space, how did he breathe? Did the clouds continue with him in space?

Underscoring the point, the astrophysicist Carl Sagan calculated that if Jesus had literally flown off into the sky, even at the speed of light (186,400 miles per second) he

---

* John Dominic Crossan, *The Power of Parable: How Fiction by Jesus Became Fiction about Jesus* (SPCK, 2012).

still wouldn't yet have made it out of our galaxy! Actually, he would still have 93,000 years to go, even to get that far. It's a silly point, I know, and Sagan had his tongue firmly pushed into his cheek, but it was meant to demonstrate how ridiculous he thought a literal belief in the ascension was.

Just imagine if the ascension happened today: would a woman walking her dog on the Mount of Olives be able to quickly grab her phone and take a picture of it; post it on Facebook? Or would the astronauts on the International Space Station be able to wave to Jesus as he passed by?

Of course not. The ascension wasn't that sort of event: a physical happening in space and time. It's a story; a very good story. But it is also a narrative device, a theological metaphor, to explain how Jesus shifted from being a historical figure living in Palestine and executed by the Romans to become a risen presence with his early followers, and subsequently with millions of people throughout history. I don't for a moment imagine that Luke thought he was describing an event that physically occurred. His understanding of truth and storytelling was more sophisticated than that of the modern-day religious and atheist literalists, who either defend it as a fact or discard it as a fairy tale.

Yet it is a story from a different era, when people thought that the world was flat, that there was an underworld where the dead went, and that heaven was a place 'out there' somewhere above the sky. Luke told a story in an idiom that made sense to him at the time. But now we have a different view of things. We know that the world is round, not flat. We know that 'up' for some people is 'down' for others. We know that, from a northern hemisphere perspective, if Jesus had left the earth from Australia he would have 'ascended' downwards; if he had left the earth from Mexico he would have gone sideways. We no longer live in a three-tier universe. We inhabit endless space with no up or down. There is no heaven as a place out there; that is a completely mistaken, literalist way to think about the world and the cosmos – about heaven.

Through the centuries there have been many artistic portrayals of the ascension of Christ. Some of them are wonderful works of art, but most of them are bizarre to the modern mind. I love the sculptured image of Christ's feet hanging from the ceiling at the Shrine of Our Lady of Walsingham, but I confess that looking at it I am always left with the sense that Jesus got stuck in the plaster while passing through.

'Ascension' is a word inescapably linked to the three-tier universe. Taken literally, it makes no sense today. That said, there is a little more to it than that, because the metaphor of *ascent* is deeply embedded in the human psyche; progress tends to be envisaged in terms of 'rising', 'ascending', 'climbing upward', 'soaring', etc. The classic idea of spiritual progress also tends to be perceived as an upward journey, never as a path of descent. People have always looked up to the skies to dream and aspire. So, yes, it feels natural to think of heaven as something 'up there', and to picture Jesus ascending to God.

While it is unlikely, therefore, that the idea of ascent will disappear from spiritual language, or from our imagination, anytime soon, it is problematic. To begin with, it suggests a form of spirituality that takes us not only towards God, but away from the world, away from nature, away from the physical creation. This has severe negative implications in an ecological age. Indeed, there is a strong argument that the spirituality of ascent, with an attendant emphasis on heaven above and the transitoriness of the material world, helped to lay the ground for the environmental crisis.

Instead of gazing upwards towards heaven, away from the world, we desperately need to look around us: to comprehend the destructiveness of our collective lifestyle to the Earth and its creatures. Instead of a God 'up there', separate from the world, we need to recognise the God who is utterly embedded in nature, the God who feels and shares in the environmental sufferings of the Earth and its creatures.

By far my favourite painting of the ascension is Salvador Dali's *The Ascension of Christ*, which implies a different metaphysical twist and points me towards a spirituality rooted in this world. Dali's mother was a Catholic, his father an atheist. Dali himself rejected an orthodox doctrinal understanding of Christianity, but he was fascinated by the mystical relationship between religion and science, and reflected this in several of his paintings.

He said his inspiration for *The Ascension of Christ* came from a 'cosmic dream' he had in 1950, some eight years prior to painting the picture. In his vividly coloured dream he saw the nucleus of an atom, with Christ moving towards it; Dali later realised that this nucleus was the true representation of the unifying spirit of Christ.

Often, 'Christ' is simply treated as a last name for Jesus, but in St Paul's letter to the Colossians, the writer presents the notion of 'Christ' as something much older and greater than the historical Jesus: 'the firstborn over all creation . . . He is before all things, and in him all things hold together.'* Christians believe that Christ was manifest in Jesus of Nazareth, but actually, the first

---

* Colossians 1:15–17.

incarnation of Christ occurred at the Big Bang 13.8 billion years ago, and from that point – through all the boundless stages of cosmic evolution – the material and the spiritual (God and creation) have always co-existed. Long before Jesus of Nazareth, God became incarnate through light and land, through sun and moon and stars, through trees and plants and birds and insects and animals. The cosmic Christ (or the unifying spirit of Christ, as Dali spoke of it) is the pervasive presence of the divine in the entire universe, right down to the atomic and subatomic.

What Dali does in his painting is to move the ascension away from a depiction of a literal event in a three-tier universe two thousand years ago, to envisage a symbolic event in which Jesus is journeying into a sunburst of energy, reaching down as he enters the nucleus of an atom, into the very ground of existence. Christ is not so much going upwards at the ascension as inwards.

The ascension may not have been a historically observable event, but it symbolised something that *did* happen. The New Testament scholar Walter Wink argued that the ascension was an event in the history of the psyche rather than on the physical plane. One of the prejudices in modern thought is the idea that real events only occur in the outer, material world, but the inner world of imagination and psychic and emotional experience is real too, and has a major effect on our outer world. The ascension was an event on the imaginal plane, and it irreversibly transformed the disciples' consciousness – and subsequently the world. It is an inner experience rather than a historical fact; something to be practised rather than simply believed in.

During their time with him, the disciples loved to watch Jesus preach, and heal and cast out demons; they delighted to be with him when he wined and dined with 'sinners' to the revulsion of the religious hoity-toity; they swelled with pride when he fearlessly confronted temple corruption by overturning the moneychangers' tables. And they wept bitterly when they saw him arrested, tried and crucified. But the ascension utterly transformed their psychic and spiritual landscape. He was no longer a localised human being – one person in one place at a time – no longer a first-century Jewish man, but a living reality everywhere.

'He is risen' has nothing to do with the resuscitation of a body now no longer needed; it is the proclamation of a new order, a new consciousness that Christ is at the core of everything, God is all and in all. In his final conversations with his disciples, Jesus told them that it was necessary for him to depart. Yes, of course it was; otherwise they would hang on to him as he was – and fail to discover the greater purpose, fail to discover Christ within themselves, within the world at large. The ultimate intention was never a unique individual walking around Galilee performing miracles, but the Spirit of Christ manifest in all the Earth – in all people.

The psychologist Carl Jung said that Christ is the God image in each of us, and that Christ would never have made the impression he did on his followers if he had not expressed something that was alive and active in their unconscious. I see this as quite similar to the Quaker belief that the light of Christ is a reality in every human being – 'there is that of God in everyone'.

To me, the ascension is the unveiling of this reality: when it dawns upon us that the cosmic Christ is the living core of everything – the one who is before all things, and in whom all things hold together – the intermingling of divinity with humanity, with all creation.

I believe that once we get past simply defending the ascension as a quirky literal fact, and allow its truth to impact us, we can recognise that it shatters every idea of an exclusive religious club, any holy huddle of 'real Christians' or 'chosen ones'. No person or group, no movement or religion, no culture or tradition, no sectional interest can own what Christ represents.

12. I believe in life before death

the afterlife is above my pay grade

It is not the end of the physical body that should worry us. Rather, our concern must be to live while we're alive.

Elizabeth Kübler-Ross

Every Sunday evening at 6.30 p.m. in the church where I grew up we would gather for the 'gospel meeting', a service where it was hoped the 'unsaved' would turn up to hear about Jesus. Mercifully for them, perhaps, they almost never did. But that didn't stop us preaching at them, all the same.

I have memories of scary sermons from visiting preachers who would warn of the perils of 'an eternity without Christ'. The fires of hell would be stoked with stern admonitions to flee the world and its sinful pleasures, and turn to Jesus. I recall creepy lines in sermons like: 'If you leave this place tonight and walk under a bus – where will you spend eternity?'

As a fifteen-year-old boy preoccupied with girls, Liverpool Football Club, The Beatles and other such 'sinful pleasures', I spent many a Sunday evening squirming in my seat, fearing for my soul's eternal well-being.

Though, actually, it wasn't so much the threat of hell that frightened me, but the promise of heaven. The thought of praying, singing hymns and worshipping for all eternity (which was all that seemed to be on offer) struck me as a pretty devastating form of everlasting torment in itself. I would sometimes even lay awake at night fretting over the terrifying prospect of living for ever and ever and ever and ever and ever – with only Christian songs and prayer meetings for entertainment. And apparently, I wasn't alone in this trepidation: I read somewhere that no less a figure than the great twentieth-century British prime minister Lloyd George once said:

When I was a boy the thought of heaven used to frighten me more than the thought of hell. I pictured heaven as a place where there would be perpetual Sundays, with perpetual services from which there would be no escape, as the Almighty, assisted by cohorts of angels, would always be on the lookout for those who did not attend.

But growing up in Liverpool in the 1960s, I soon became far too busy enjoying *this* world to worry about the next. The atmosphere in the city at that time pulsated with new sounds, new fashions, new ideas and new experiences. I felt I was at the centre of the universe. As far as I was concerned, heaven couldn't hold a candle to what I had right there.

I am sure that my religious upbringing was quite extreme. There are many other more nuanced versions of heaven and hell, yet a large chunk of popular Christian teaching still focuses on the issue of the afterlife, and the importance of making sure that you will land up in the right place when you die.

As for me, decades after squirming in those 'gospel meetings', I confess I am still very much at home in *this* world. I have no hankering for 'a home beyond the blue' or the equivalent. This is where I belong. I am an earthling: a bit-part player in 4.5 billion years of breath-taking evolutionary history. Like everyone else, my entire existence is intricately knitted into Earth's vast and complex web of life and relationships.

It's not just history that ties us to this planet; we share in its future too. The universe is still coming into being, the adventure continues. And we human beings are part of it. If there is a destiny for humanity in God's eternal purpose, which I believe there is, it can only be as part of the greater destiny of God for the Earth, the cosmos and the whole of creation. This includes the world of nature too, and billions of stars and galaxies flung across space – and their possible inhabitants. The question of what meaning my little life may have is intrinsically tied up with the meaning and destiny of all creation.

This is not, however, the vision of Christianity most of us have inherited. The widespread impression is that Christianity centres on one miniscule fragment of the universe's story, the only bit that counts, apparently: human history, and in particular human salvation, which in popular perception means going to heaven instead of hell when we die.

My first major problem with this vision of Christianity is that it is horribly anthropocentric. The world, though a magnificent creation of God, basically serves as a mere backdrop to the drama of God's dealings with humanity. It has no ultimate value or purpose of its own. Which is why many Christians think that 'saving souls' is far more important than saving the planet: souls are eternal but the planet is finally disposable. But what about the rest of creation: where does that fit in? And what about the other 14 billion years of cosmic history – was God just sitting around waiting for human history to begin? I can't imagine that the God of the universe would be so species prejudiced as to not include the whole of Earth's creaturely community plus whatever/whoever else lives out there in the further reaches of the cosmos.

And then there is the problem of heaven and hell. I long ago gave up belief in anything resembling the notion of hell that I grew up with. The concept of people suffering for eternity because they didn't believe in Jesus (or even if they committed horrendous crimes against humanity) has to be one of the most brutally psychotic ideas ever imagined, and certainly unworthy of any faith claiming to worship a God of love.

Apart from anything else, how could eternal torment and eternal bliss co-exist? Surely, the one obliterates the other. What sort of people could party for ever while others suffered interminable misery? What sort of God would preside over such a state of affairs? The God of Jesus Christ would surely rescue the tormented even if it took all eternity. The popular notion of hell is an affront to spiritual intelligence.

Even if eternal torment were plainly in the Bible, I would oppose it in the name of God. But it isn't in the Bible. As Jon Sweeney has persuasively argued, the popular notion of hell is really the product of the medieval imagination, spectacularly articulated in Dante's *Inferno*, but now so embedded in Christian myth that it is routinely read back into biblical texts even though closer examination reveals that it isn't there.*

The New Testament scholar Marcus Borg is convinced that an emphasis on the afterlife distorts Christianity and what it's about. I agree. It isn't that I don't believe in an afterlife. It is just that once we make the afterlife the emphasis, it *mostly* turns Christianity into a reward and punishment religion; it *mostly* creates an 'us and them' mentality – the 'saved' and the 'unsaved'; it *mostly* takes attention away from this world to what may lie ahead; and it *mostly* focuses on the self – how can I be spared from hell?

---

* Jon M. Sweeney, *Inventing Hell: Dante, the Bible, and Eternal Torment* (Jericho Books, 2014). I have expanded on my own disbelief in hell in *Re-Enchanting Christianity* (Canterbury Press, 2008).

My understanding of Christianity is that it centres on divine grace – God's unconditional love, which knows nothing of restricted entry: believe this, or do that, or join us and then you will be saved. The only sort of afterlife that I can believe in is one where God's love ultimately encompasses all, includes all, reconciles all.

There is a wartime story about some soldiers in France who brought the body of a comrade to a church cemetery to be buried. The priest asked whether the man was a baptised Catholic. The men didn't know, didn't care; he was their friend. The priest told them that sadly he could not bury the body in the graveyard without being sure. So the soldiers dug a grave just outside the fence of the grave-yard, and buried him there. The next day they returned with some flowers but couldn't find the grave. Apparently the priest, troubled by his refusal to bury the man, had been unable to sleep. Early in the morning he went to the cemetery and moved the fence so that it included the grave of the soldier.

For me, this is an excellent picture of grace. Segregation is the antithesis of everything I comprehend of God. As a Jew living in Judea, Jesus mostly encountered his own people, but when he did interact with non-Jews, he never condemned or rejected them, never showed the slightest inclination to try to convert them, never required them to believe the 'right' things in order to be accepted. Jesus had no 'club' for people to join, no creed for them to sign up to. He simply called people to follow him, to be part of his way.

Eternal life in the teaching of Jesus is not about an afterlife, but about a quality of life here and now rooted in justice, peace and liberation. He invited his listeners to ditch their greedy, selfish, violent, ego-driven existence and discover a life of love, forgiveness, generosity and healing.

When Jesus invited himself to the home of Zacchaeus, a swindling tax collector, for a nice cup of tea, it resulted in a total change of heart for Zacchaeus. He promised, 'Look, Lord! Here and now I give half of my possessions to the poor, and if I have cheated anybody out of anything, I will pay back four times the amount.' Jesus responded, 'Today salvation has come to this house.'* Salvation had nothing to do with an afterlife experience for Zacchaeus. It was about a present reality: a new quality of life that *saved* him from the misery of greed, selfishness and consequent loneliness.

On another occasion, a wealthy man asked Jesus what he must do to inherit eternal life. Jesus told him to keep

---

* Luke 19:1–10.

the commandments, and also to sell his goods and distribute the takings among the poor. If it were not Jesus who said this, many modern Christians would say he was wrong. Salvation is by faith, not good works, they would argue. But Jesus wasn't talking about earning salvation; he was describing what salvation looks like as a life practice. A life of goodness, unselfishness and compassion is a 'saved' life, whereas greed, indifference and self-righteousness lead to a life 'lost'.

Is there an afterlife? I don't know. And if you are honest, neither do you. No one knows. We may believe deeply and sincerely that there is an afterlife, but that doesn't make it true. We may quote Bible verses or teachings of the Church, but these are not proof, however convinced we may be about them.

I meet people all the time who assure me that they know for certain what will happen when we die. And I don't simply mean Christians: some atheist friends have absolutely no doubt that we will all simply rot in the ground. End of story! But actually, none of us can know for sure, because none of us has been there yet. And, certainly, believing that there is some kind of life after life is no less intellectually defensible than believing that we simply decay.

What we can know for sure is that there is life *before* death. We all have choices about how to live that life:

whether to behave as though everything revolved around 'me', or to genuinely care about others; whether to abuse the Earth and its creatures, or to respect the world as kith and kin; whether to be driven by the ego, or be animated and directed by love.

A young Christian man recently asked me, 'But if there is no afterlife, why wouldn't I just drink and take drugs and have sex with everyone?' It's a revealing question, but it's not a stupid one. I have been asked something very similar by much more mature Christians. One lady told me, 'If we can't be absolutely certain about going to heaven when we die, then why would we bother?' Another person said, 'If I do end up simply rotting in the ground, then faith will have been a sick joke!'

Such reactions simply underscore my point: that an emphasis on the afterlife distorts the message of Christianity and what it is about. Surely, Jesus calls us primarily to a way of life, a way of being in the world. Do we really need the prospect of punishment or reward to make good decisions in life? Is that all that believing in God or following Jesus amounts to – a guarantee of living for ever? If that is how it works, then I will probably give it a miss. I know atheists with not a care about a blessed afterlife who effectively choose to live the Jesus way, sacrificing wealth and comfort, and even life itself, for things that they believe to be more important than personal survival.

The fact is, if eternal life is a quality of life that begins now, then many atheists and agnostics as well as people of various faiths have already inherited eternal life: the man who gave a kidney to a total stranger; the woman who sacrificed a successful career to be an aid worker in Syria; the person who volunteered to work in a care home every weekend; the woman who offers meals to lonely people in her neighbourhood. These apparently faithless people whom I feel proud to know are living eternal life right now.

The question 'If there is no hell or heaven, why be a Christian?' makes no sense to the spiritually intelligent. A life of goodness, love and altruism stems from deeply held values and attitudes that we choose to adopt and internalise because we know that they are right. They have nothing to do with reward and punishment. Isn't this what Jesus actually meant when he said that we should give alms in secret: that the reward is in doing what we know to be right, not in receiving praise or reimbursement of some kind?

I do believe in an afterlife. I can't prove it. I may turn out to be wrong. But that is OK, because even if I could be convinced that everything simply ends at death, I would not live any other way. I would continue to follow the way of Jesus as best I could, because that is the kind of human being I want to be.

What does life beyond death mean? I cannot finally say. But I cannot imagine that it equates with any descriptions I have heard of it. Surely, the afterlife is a mystery, and I am happy to keep it that way. Like the poet Mary Oliver, I want to step through the door of death full of curiosity, wondering what it is going to be like, that 'cottage of darkness'. Her poem 'When Death Comes' isn't really about death, but about living in the present: treating all living creatures as brothers and sisters, embracing the world lovingly in our arms, behaving courageously and not fearfully – ensuring that we really *live* and not merely exist.

I am inclined to think of heaven as a parallel reality, or a different state of consciousness, rather than as a place. If heaven is where God is, then heaven is as close as God, and nothing is closer to us than God. Therefore, the dead are not distant, but present alongside us. And death is just another step of evolution.

The writer John O'Donohue reminds us that the oldest and most beautiful metaphor to convey this process is the journey of the larva to become a butterfly. Once the larva becomes a butterfly it cannot go back and re-enter the world of the larva. As a larva it was bound to the earth and water, but now as a butterfly it inhabits the air. It can fly overhead, look down and remember where and who it was, but not even for a second can it return to that existence.*

How true John O'Donohue's description is, I cannot say. I do believe that metaphors and poetic imagination get us closer to an understanding of death and the after-life than any attempts at literal descriptions. As a vicar taking funerals and supporting the bereaved, I speak all the time with people who sense very forcibly the presence of departed loved ones and relate amazing stories of how this has an impact on their lives.

When all is said and done, however, the afterlife really is above my pay grade. I can quote verses from the Bible, repeat Christian mantras passed down through the ages, share my experiences, thoughts and hunches, say what others tell me, but actually I don't know. At one time, this might have troubled me, but as time passes I become less bothered about what happens when I die and much more bothered about how I am living now. The best way I know to prepare for death and the hereafter is to

* John O'Donohue, *Divine Beauty: The Invisible Embrace* (Bantam Press, 2003).

cultivate and intensify our relationship with life, with the whole cosmic and physical reality of here and now, and to live faithfully and authentically with the things we sense most strongly in the depths of our being. Spiritual intelligence thrives on authenticity.

Julia was one of the most authentic people I have known. She wasn't just a member of my church, she was a dear friend who finally lost her life to cancer, aged forty-eight, after living with it for twelve years. She couldn't remember how many operations she had undergone; how many dozens of specialists had treated her. No one expected her to live that long. She was a skinny slip of a thing, but had a heart the size of Mount Everest. Anyone who enquired about her well-being would quickly find the question reversed: 'But how are you?' It wasn't a deflection tactic but a genuine expression of concern from one of God's kindliest.

Julia taught me two things, that's all: how to die and how to live. She always knew the disease would get her in the end, but she never feared it, never gave it the opportunity to stop her living every day as fully and completely as she possibly could. She entrusted herself to the Spirit of life that can only be found in the present moment.

A few months before she died, while she still had the strength, Julia and her husband went on a wonderful holiday where she got up in the morning and did whatever she wanted. She swam in the sea, went for walks, climbed, and laughed a lot – which she was very good at.

The truth is, I still want to run a mile from death, but Julia taught me not to live in fear, because fear paralyses. While we fear, we cannot experience joy or beauty or love; fear contracts the soul into a black hole of sleepy existence. Julia taught me to live in faith: to trust myself into the adventure of life, come what may; to value every stone on the road, even the jagged rocks that hurt the feet. Because this is life, the only life we have.

Letting go is one of the hardest things to do in life, but it is also the most important. And letting go of life is the hardest thing of all. A couple of months before she died, Julia came to see me. She knew time was short. She told me that whatever lay ahead, she did not regret a thing. Her life wasn't perfect, but she felt content. 'It's time to let go, Dave,' she said.

On the morning when I kissed Julia for the last time on the day she died, and read Psalm 23 to her – 'Though I walk through the valley of the shadow of death, I will fear no evil, for you are with me' – I knew her life on Earth was complete, but I had the distinct impression that, for her, the adventure was actually just beginning.

Maybe there is a heaven. I think there is. But I want to forget about it now, and simply get on with living. I want to live a life I will look back on from my deathbed and say, 'Wow! What a ride!'

And then see what comes next.

13. I believe God is human

it's the rest of us I'm not sure about

Religion has a future only if it shows its philan-
thropic face, an inviting face, and not caricatured
and repellent features.

Hans Küng

When a friend asked if we would like Hans Küng to come to
the vicarage for dinner, I almost collapsed with excitement.

Hans Küng is one of the greatest Christian thinkers of
our time, and an architect of the modernising second

201

Vatican Council that transformed the Catholic Church in the early 1960s (though he was later censured by the Vatican for being too liberal).

Küng was born in Switzerland in 1928. In his mid-twenties he was ordained as a priest in the Catholic Church, and at the amazingly young age of thirty-one became a professor of theology at Tübingen University in Germany, where he has pursued his entire academic career. For a scholar, he is outrageously readable, with over seventy books to his credit, many of them bestsellers. He addressed the UN General Assembly shortly after 9/11 on the future of international relations, and served on a twenty-person 'Group of Eminent Persons' set up by Kofi Annan. He is a friend to many heads of government and leaders of the world religions, and has more academic and humanitarian awards than you can shake a stick at.

Küng is a rock star in the world of global theology. Yet in the eyes of the conservative Catholic establishment, he is a black sheep, a subversive rebel and free-thinker who has to be silenced. Over the decades he has challenged the authority of the Pope, argued in favour of gay relationships, canvassed for women priests, stated that if Jesus of Nazareth returned he would welcome divorcees into the Church, described the Vatican's prohibition on birth control as pernicious, and encouraged Catholic parishes to keep their priests after they marry even if church law declares they are no longer priests.

Hans Küng is one of my heroes. The prospect of entertaining him in our home was both delightful and terrifying. Pat shared my excitement, but was characteristically less star struck. When I showed her my copy of Küng's *Does God Exist?* she flicked through the nine hundred pages and commented wryly, 'Is that a yes, then?' However, she loves a good story, and Hans had plenty of them to tell.

I'm not sure how accustomed the Herr Professor was to sitting at a family table, but after an extra helping of roast dinner he relaxed, and talked freely about his fascinating life and his relationship with Pope John XXIII, who initiated Vatican II but sadly died before it was completed. We also discussed the then Cardinal Joseph Ratzinger (later Pope Benedict XVI), who played a significant part in barring Küng's teaching from the Church in 1979. And we had fun quizzing him about what would be the first things he would change if he were Pope (dumping enforced celibacy for priests figured high on the list).

After dinner, I jumped at Küng's offer to sign my copies of his books. But when Pat handed him *Does God Exist?*, pointing to the title, I knew exactly what was coming next: 'Is that a yes then, Hans?' I held my breath, certain that no one had ever put the question to him in quite that fashion. A broad grin shot across his wrinkled face, then on the opening page he wrote: 'Yes! Read it!' My wife, always one to have the last word, impishly responded, 'Well, I don't really need to now that you've told me the answer!'

One of the topics I was eager to discuss with Hans Küng was his work on the 'global ethic': the creation of a consensus among the world's religions on a set of shared ethical values, standards and attitudes.

'The world is torn apart by politics and religion,' he told me. 'We must learn to live together peacefully, and share responsibility in caring for the earth and for each other . . . we need a basic moral code, a global ethic.' While he never saw the global ethic as an exclusively religious affair – he always wanted an alliance of believers and non-believers – Küng was convinced that the religions must lead the way, not least because religion is implicit in so many of the world's conflicts and problems. In my copy of *Yes to a Global Ethic* he inscribed his oft-repeated dictum:

> No peace among the nations
> without peace among the religions;

No peace among the religions
without dialogue between the religions.

The central plank of the global ethic is the so-called
'golden rule', some version of which can be found in every
religious tradition: 'Do not treat others as you would not
like them to treat you', or, in its positive form, 'In everything do to others as you would have them do to you.'

The Golden Rule in World Religions

Hinduism
*This is the sum of duty: do not do to others what
would cause pain if done to you.*

Baha'i
*Ascribe not to any soul that which thou wouldst not
have ascribed to thee.*

Islam
That which you want for yourself, seek for mankind.

Buddhism
*Hurt not others in ways that you yourself would find
hurtful.*

Confucianism

Do not impose on others what you do not yourself desire.

Judaism

Love your neighbour as yourself.

Christianity

In everything do to others as you would have them do to you.

Taoism

Regard your neighbour's gain as your own gain, and your neighbour's loss as your own loss.

Sikhism

Never impose on others what you would not choose for yourself.

Zoroastrianism

Whatever is disagreeable to yourself do not do unto others.

At the 1993 Parliament of the World's Religions in Chicago, more than two hundred leaders from over forty different faith traditions signed a 'Declaration toward a Global Ethic', drafted by Hans Küng. In essence it calls for a more humane world based on the assumption that 'every person without distinction of age, sex, race, skin colour, physical or mental ability, language, religion, political view, or national or social origin possesses an inalienable and untouchable dignity, and everyone, the individual as well as the state, is therefore obliged to honour this dignity and protect it'.

Before drafting the declaration, Küng spent time listening to representatives of many different religions and cultures around the world and concluded that there are four funda-mental, universal ethical imperatives: 'Do not murder, do not steal, do not lie, do not misuse sexuality.' Reinterpreted and applied to the contemporary context, Küng made these the basis for his draft declaration, which calls upon every person, institution and nation to take responsibility for creating:

1. A culture of non-violence and respect for all life – 'do not murder'.
2. A culture of solidarity and a just economic order – 'do not steal'.
3. A culture of tolerance and a life of truthfulness – 'do not lie'.
4. A culture of equal rights and partnership between men and women – 'do not misuse sexuality'.*

* See the full text of the declaration at http://cchu9014.weebly.com/uploads/1/6/2/0/16200980/towardsaglobalethic.pdf.

Despite being signed in 1993, far from losing any of its relevance, the declaration has rather gained added potency, especially since 9/11. But also since the global economic crash in 2008, which Küng predicted a decade earlier. Behind the economic crisis, he maintains, is a crisis of ethics. Ethics and economics need to be reintegrated: an ethic that lacks any economic dimension lapses into gutless moralism, while a culture of success devoid of ethical restraint results in anti-social consequences for countless people as well as the planet. Only with some elementary ethical norms, as they have developed since the human race began, can self-destructive human greed and vanity be tamed for the good of the whole Earth community.

In 2008 Hans Küng was awarded the Otto Hahn Peace Medal in Berlin for 'exemplary commitment to humanity, tolerance and dialogue between the great world religions above all in the framework of the Global Ethic project'.

In his ceremonial speech, Küng took the opportunity to stress to his predominantly secular audience his belief that the global ethic need not be grounded in the religions. Endorsing the humanist claim that 'you don't need God to be good', he sketched out a philosophical basis for a global ethic that had no necessary reliance on religious beliefs.

The real distinction, highlighted by Küng's global ethic, is not between people who are religious and people who are not, or between those who adhere to this faith or that, but between the practice of compassion and empathy and a culture of greed, selfishness and inhumanity. There are people of all religions and none who pursue both of these paths. No individual or group has a corner on either goodness or stupidity.

It is very clear that Confucius, the Buddha, Jesus of Nazareth and the Prophet Mohammed were all strong advocates of humanity and of a more humane world. Also that, despite massive differences, humanist ethics and the ethics of the world religions converge significantly on a basic understanding of what it means to be truly human.

Like Hans Küng, I describe myself as both a Christian and a humanist. I see no inherent conflict between the two things. Indeed, I am convinced that Christianity is intrinsically humanistic, especially when viewed through the lens of Jesus of Nazareth and the golden rule.

As a Christian and a humanist:

- I believe that *our most basic reality is that we are earthlings* who share in the 4.6-billion-year sacred story of planetary evolution. We are intricately interconnected with the whole biosphere and its creatures, and in an age of ecological crisis we must establish sustainable environmental policies and practices for the good of all.

- I believe that regardless of differences of religion, gender, ethnicity, skin colour, sexual orientation, social status, etc., *what unites us most fundamentally is a common humanity*. First, and most fundamentally, I am a human being, and then a Christian only by choice. The greatest threat to the world lies in the refusal of many to honour this essential fact and therefore to respect difference.

- I believe in *the value and dignity of each person*; that there is 'that of God' in everyone, and therefore every human being deserves to be valued and accorded the greatest possible freedom that is compatible with the rights of others.

- I believe that *morality is an intrinsic part of human nature*; that a person does not need to be religious in order to have morals and ethics – you don't need God to be good!

- I believe in *the absolute freedom of rational enquiry*; that no belief, creed or conviction should be beyond question. All truth is God's truth no matter where it is found. There is therefore no necessary conflict between science and religion, between reason and faith. God and evolution gave us the capacity to observe and reflect, to doubt and question, to listen and discuss and then decide; it would be rude (and stupid) not to use that capacity as fully as we can.

- I believe in democracy, human rights and the maximum possible conditions for human development, and consequently, that *it is our responsibility to seek justice and equality for every person*, to ensure that everyone's voice is heard.

- I believe that *personal liberty must be combined with social responsibility*; that we may vigorously disagree with others, but never bully or attempt to coerce them into agreement. I believe in a society where vastly different creeds and worldviews can co-exist peacefully in mutual respect.

- Finally, I believe that *these beliefs – that all beliefs – are worthless unless they support and lead us into the practice of treating others as we ourselves wish to be treated*. This is not only at the heart of all religion, but also at the core of what it means to be human.

While Jesus never explicitly voiced these proposals, I am convinced they represent in modern form and idiom the sort of values and priorities that he embodied and proclaimed in the Gospels. For example:

- He constantly affirmed the dignity and value of people who were marginalised and stigmatised in his society: women, children, immigrants, so-called sinners and the ritually unclean.
- He boiled the 613 laws from the Hebrew Bible down to just two basic essentials: love God with all you are, and love your neighbour as yourself.
- He taught people to critically evaluate the religious dogmas of the day, and to look to the heart of their religion instead of worrying about rules and conventions.
- At the same time as being kind and generous towards the poor, the excluded and the defamed, he relentlessly criticised the wealthy and the powerful, and especially the self-serving religious establishment.
- He denounced nationalism and tribalism, often making foreigners and social misfits the heroes of his stories. He commended reaching out to strangers, and taught us to love our enemies.

- He condemned social injustice and greed, and called on the wealthy and influential to use their privilege to benefit others.
- He gave a voice to the voiceless, and stood up for the rights of those who had no rights.
- He said that the way we treat other people directly reflects the actual nature of our religion.

These are the kinds of things that make me a follower of Jesus, which keep me on the Christian path when I am tempted to give it up. I have no difficulty with Jesus as the decisive revelation of God in human form, but frankly, I get bored with fourth-century convoluted arguments about the deity of Christ. What I and others want is to push the world in a more humane direction. For that task we seek a Jesus who is not an omnipotent God in a man-suit, but someone like us, who looked for God at the centre of his life and called the world to join him; who is the model of what it is to be human, and showed us the humanity of God.

My personal notion of humanism is firmly grounded in what Jesus called the kingdom of God, especially in his explanation of this in the Sermon on the Mount. The kingdom of God is not a code of ethics or a detailed programme of action, but the promise of a humane world when we rediscover the heart of God in the depths of humanity and set about building our lives and communities around that.

Of course, Christians do not have a monopoly on this. A similar concept to the kingdom of God exists in the Jewish ethic of *tikkun olam*, which literally means 'repair the world'. During the sixteenth century, in the Galilean village of Tsefat, Rabbi Isaac Luria observed that the world had many things wrong. There was hunger, war, disease and hatred. 'How could God allow such things?' people wondered. 'Perhaps it is because God needs our help,' Luria responded. And he explained his answer with the following mystical legend.

When the world was first made, God planned to pour light into everything to make it real and alive. But something went wrong. The light was so bright that the vessels containing it burst, shattering into millions of broken pieces. Our world is such a mess because it is filled with broken fragments. When people fight and hurt each other, they allow the world to stay shattered. 'We live in a cosmic heap of broken pieces, and God cannot fix it alone,' Luria said.

That is why God created us and gave us freedom of choice. We are free to do whatever we choose with the world. We can allow things to remain broken, or we can join with God in repairing them. Whether we call it *tikkun olam*, as Rabbi Luria did, or the kingdom of God, or Christ-inspired humanism, our task remains the same: to share a co-responsibility with God and each other to bring healing and wholeness to the world.

When I recently talked about the global ethic to a class of students in a local school, one young man asked if there was anything he could do to support it. A fellow student immediately replied that we can all do small things to help with the task: support humane causes on change.org, give to charitable causes, spread kindness in our daily life, befriend people who are alone or bullied, make sure our garden is hospitable to wildlife. Listening to her reply increased my faith that future generations may do better than mine.

The Charter for Compassion is a more recent initiative than the global ethic, aimed at restoring compassion to our public and religious life. I encourage you to sign the charter, maybe create a 'charter salon' or a 'compassionate community'.* Take a few moments to reflect on the charter:

> The principle of compassion lies at the heart of all religious, ethical and spiritual traditions, calling us

---

* See https://www.charterforcompassion.org.

always to treat all others as we wish to be treated ourselves. Compassion impels us to work tirelessly to alleviate the suffering of our fellow creatures, to dethrone ourselves from the centre of our world and put another there, and to honour the inviolable sanctity of every single human being, treating everybody, without exception, with absolute justice, equity and respect.

It is also necessary in both public and private life to refrain consistently and empathically from inflicting pain. To act or speak violently out of spite, chauvinism, or self-interest, to impoverish, exploit or deny basic rights to anybody, and to incite hatred by denigrating others – even our enemies – is a denial of our common humanity. We acknowledge that we have failed to live compassionately and that some have even increased the sum of human misery in the name of religion.

We therefore call upon all men and women to restore compassion to the centre of morality and religion ~ to return to the ancient principle that any interpretation of scripture that breeds violence, hatred or disdain is illegitimate ~ to ensure that youth are given accurate and respectful information about other traditions, religions and cultures ~ to encourage a positive appreciation of cultural and religious diversity ~ to cultivate an informed empathy with the suffering of all human beings – even those regarded as enemies.

We urgently need to make compassion a clear, luminous and dynamic force in our polarized world. Rooted in a principled determination to transcend selfishness, compassion can break down political, dogmatic, ideological and religious boundaries. Born of our deep interdependence, compassion is essential to human relationships and to a fulfilled humanity. It is the path to enlightenment, and indispensable to the creation of a just economy and a peaceful global community.

It is true that compassion lies at the heart of every religion, but every religion also contains elements which are less than compassionate, and in some instances, downright inhumane. And herein lies the task of every religious tradition: to evolve or reform our religious beliefs and practices to become more humane and benevolent. It's a process that reactionary religious devotees often brand as 'liberal', by which they mean unfaithful to the sacred texts and traditions, or departing from the truth, while in fact it is simply an outworking of the golden rule – a radical willingness to place oneself in the shoes of the other person.

Far from seeing humanism as an enemy of faith, or as anti-God, I see it as an essential ingredient of faith, as a way of drawing closer to the God we only really know in human form.

14. I believe in Hobnobs, beer and round tables
church for misfits, black sheep and prodigals

The world come of age is more god-less and perhaps just because of that closer to God than the world not yet come of age.

Dietrich Bonhoeffer

Seven-year-old William couldn't believe it when his favourite biscuits turned up on the Communion plate.

It was an occasion when the bishop was visiting (would you believe it!). He preached, and I officiated at the

Eucharist. Then we joined together to administer Communion. Everything was going swimmingly, until part way through serving Communion I realised that with a packed church I had miscalculated and did not have enough bread for the remaining people in the line.

Since the solution to most predicaments in my life is called 'Pat', I gestured to her to bring a fresh supply. There was none. So, to everyone's delight (and no one's great surprise), grinning from ear to ear, my beloved traipsed forward with a plate of Hobnob biscuits – right under the nose of the bishop. Fortunately, he is a man with a healthy sense of humour.

Undeterred, I went ahead and consecrated the biscuits, then continued offering Communion. One by one, people came forward, beaming as I placed a piece of broken biscuit on their outstretched palms: 'The body of Christ.'

William's mum later told me that for some weeks he insisted on holding back at Communion just in case the Hobnobs made a fresh appearance. So far, they haven't . . . but never say never, William.

To some people, Hobnobs for Communion will seem bizarre and irreverent; blasphemous, even. But I consecrated those biscuits with all the joyous dignity I bring to the usual loaf of bread purchased from the same supermarket. I don't imagine Hobnobs will be standard fare at our altar any time soon, but they definitely conjured up a magical moment that no one will forget – especially William. And I don't recall Jesus banning Hobnobs at the Last Supper. Do you?

Besides, the only basis I can comprehend for believing that God is present in a pinch of bread and a sip of wine at Communion is the much broader principle that the whole Earth, the entire universe, is a sacrament; that to receive one tiny crumb of creation as the body of Christ is to affirm Christ in every part. Therefore, a Hobnob, a gingernut, a chunk of wholemeal bread, and even an ecclesiastical wafer with a cross imprinted on it may equally communicate divine grace when received with gratitude and mindfulness.

'That couldn't happen in my church,' one visitor wrote afterwards. 'The vicar and the church wardens would have kittens if someone produced Hobnobs for Communion. But it seemed delightfully natural in your church. I was one of the people who received the biscuity body of Christ. And it was probably the most meaningful experience of Communion I have had in thirty-five years!'

I think the reason why such a novel event felt so natural at St Luke's is because we have more than our share of people who like things to be a little offbeat or unconventional. We are a black sheep sort of church. Not that

221

being different is, in itself, a virtue; it may be nothing more than a mark of obstinacy or eccentricity. Yet surprise elements and playful juxtapositions can powerfully open up new perceptions, new experiences, while humdrum routine often puts people to sleep – on the inside, if not the outside.

I feel particularly aware of this at services where there are lots of non-churchgoers; at a wedding, for example, where many people see the church service as something to endure before escaping to the fun part at the reception. But a dash of humour or a novel element in a service can make a massive difference. At one recent wedding, the best man surprised us all by handing me two Hula-Hoops (circular crisps) when I asked him for the rings. Muffled laughs from the congregation signalled uncertainty about how I would respond. I blessed the Hoops, then invited the bride and groom to exchange and eat them. Everyone burst into spontaneous applause. And the happy couple enjoyed a hilariously holy moment of 'nuptial Communion'.

As the cultural historian Johan Huizinga revealed, back in the mists of time religion emerged from the human capacity for play.* Which makes me wonder why the two

---

* Johan Huizinga, *Homo Ludens: A Study of the Play-Element in Culture* (Angelico Press, 2016).

things have become such poor bedfellows. Jesus himself was the embodiment of festivity and satire – the holy fool who partied with outcasts, turned water into wine and flouted rigid tradition. When I read of him refusing to ritually wash his hands before eating in a Pharisee's house, or breaking the Sabbath day rules, or entertaining publicans and prostitutes, then I have no difficulty imagining him passing around Hobnobs at Communion or playfully inviting a bride and groom to exchange Hula-Hoops.

Black sheep and prodigals have been my travelling companions for as long as I can recall. We attract each other; a fact which has sometimes got me into trouble. I have been variously castigated, vilified and cut off for hanging out with, or defending, the wrong people. On one occasion, my main financial patrons threatened that if I continued to stick with one particular 'sinner', they would cut off my support. 'It's either him or us,' they announced.

'Well, I hope we can keep in touch,' I replied.

Holy Joes, the 'church' I led in a pub in the 1990s, was expressly designed for people who were variously bored, disenchanted, angry, disappointed or hurt by their experiences of church and Christianity. We never had services as such, but offered space for honest expression, where people could argue, doubt and question without being

223

put right by the end of the evening. Some of our regulars were pushy and hard to shut up, others needed teasing out; some wanted heady discussion, others welcomed the chance to vent their spleen. Week in, week out, every Tuesday night for ten years, we wrestled with whatever it was about church or faith that got people's goat – always with passion, never without beer and laughter and irreverent banter . . . and occasionally, a tear or two.

Many hundreds of people passed through Holy Joes during those ten years. Some came for a few weeks: 'to detox from the Church', as one person put it. Others stayed for months or years. It became a beacon of hope for misfitting spiritual travellers. One person told me, 'Holy Joes was my last chance saloon before giving up on the whole damn thing. Then I found I didn't need to.'

Tuesday nights in The Hope & Anchor pub (and The Alexandra, The Black Bull and The Railway) were almost like a twelve-step programme for religious fugitives. Our opening ritual at each meeting was to go around the room and introduce ourselves. I recall one man mischievously announcing, 'Hello, my name is Edward, I am a recovering Christian. I haven't been to a church service for nineteen months.'

I am well acquainted with the spiritual, emotional and intellectual struggles of the religiously disenchanted.

Countless hours have been spent with people whose faith has unravelled and they don't know if it can ever be knitted back together. Sometimes, vicars and church ministers will take me out for a drink, or walk me around the park, to offload their spiritual doubts and struggles: things they find it impossible to share with their congregations or colleagues.

Of course, I have my own troubling uncertainties. I sometimes tell an audience that if anyone is short of doubts or questions they can see me afterwards; I have plenty to go around. But then faith is not about certainty, not about abandoning one's critical faculties or arriving at a final outcome. Faith is messy and ambiguous. At best, my own beliefs are interim markers, stammering efforts at truth which I will probably revise . . . and then revise again. As I see it, faith is a passionate inner conversation, an internal argument between belief and doubt. Sometimes belief seems to prevail, at other times doubt, but the important thing is to keep the conversation going. Once it stops, once belief or doubt eliminates the other, then we plunge into either disbelief or certainty, neither of which gets us very far on the spiritual journey.

Frankly, I find plenty about Christianity and church to fill me with frustration and despair. I was once asked to speak to a gathering of pagans in a pub for eight minutes on the topic 'What I don't like about Christianity'. Eight minutes! How could I possibly fit it into just eight minutes?

Yet for all that, I remain committed first and foremost to Jesus Christ who constantly warms and reconverts my heart, but also to the Church, and to an understanding that community is essential to the faith process – being black sheep doesn't mean we have to be loners.

And despite my best efforts to squeeze all my doubts into eight minutes, one of the pagans told me afterwards that I had restored her faith in Christ – that she felt she could now be a Christian pagan!

If I were to boil down to a single issue all the disquiet and discontent with religion and the Church that I encounter in people, it would be the desire for a more grown-up approach to faith. They are tired of religion that is too prescribed, too done and dusted, too dominated by spiritual know-alls. People repeatedly say that they feel patronised or treated like naughty children when they don't fit in, or when they ask 'disruptive' questions or take a different point of view – as if their opinions, their moral judgements, their life choices don't count.

'In the rest of my life, people respect my ideas and decisions, even when they disagree,' a woman told me. 'But at church it feels as if there is either "truth" or "error", and I always seem to fall down on the wrong side of that particular divide. But who gets to decide? Don't I have the right to an opinion too? I'm fifty-two, for God's sake! Please treat me like an adult!'

The world outside the Church is now inherently pluralistic: all kinds of beliefs and lifestyles exist side by side. We are relentlessly exposed to a wealth of perceptions and ideas which we are expected to weigh up and then decide upon for ourselves. Talk shows, television and radio debates, phone-ins, and most of all social media and the Internet, constantly unleash upon us a tsunami of views and opinions. The world has become a clamouring exchange, a multilogue of ideas and perspectives. Little wonder, then, that people turn away from a church or religious system which they sense to be an overbearing monologue.

In earlier times, authoritarian religious discourse worked: the Church dictated what people would believe, and how they would behave, and on the whole people accepted it. But those days are long gone. As far back as the 1940s, the German theologian Dietrich Bonhoeffer observed that the old 'religious consciousness' was being replaced with a new emerging consciousness, a 'world come of age' that no longer leaned on old certainties.

By 'religious consciousness', Bonhoeffer referred to a worldview based on the authority of the Church and religion, where 'God' was the answer to all the important questions. But the world was becoming more adult, Bonhoeffer argued: not in the sense of being more mature, or even necessarily of being a better place, but in the sense of no longer needing the crutch of religion and God.

In practice, a 'world come of age' means that we now look to science to explain things, not religion; that truth is a matter of reason instead of revelation, and morality is a conversation rather than a monologue to which people are supposed to pay attention. The cat is out of the bag where religious authority is concerned; people will make up their own minds now. The monologue may continue, but fewer and fewer people will listen.

This is the situation in the Western world, where the overwhelming majority of people are now prodigals to conventional faith and churchgoing. They will no longer be told by the religious establishment what to believe or how to behave. Its voice is marginal and largely ignored.

Yet, crucially, people are no less spiritual, no less concerned to live meaningfully, no less open to truthful existence, no less eager to do the right thing. Indeed, contrary to many expectations, a 'world come of age' has led to a greater preoccupation with spiritual concerns, even if not in a conventionally religious sense. Spirituality is thriving, while religion is at best irrelevant, and at worst seen to be dangerous.

Perhaps anticipating the revived curiosity in spirituality, Bonhoeffer argued that a 'world come of age' would give birth to a 'religionless Christianity': a faith or spiritual experience outside the bubble of prescribed religion, a way of discovering God (by whatever name or label) in the very midst of life instead of a religious ghetto. People may even live without any belief in God, Bonhoeffer stated, yet still be following the way of Christ.

Religionless Christianity amounts to something very similar to what I have elsewhere described as being a 'bad Christian': *a person who shies away from organised religion, who has little time for creeds and doctrines and churchgoing, yet who lives in the spirit of Christianity or true religion.**

It is perfectly clear to me that the widespread decline of churchgoing Christianity does not represent a loss of spiritual experience or spiritual aspiration. Many people who have no religious affiliation and find no reason to seek it pursue meaning, purpose and integrity in their lives. Some may label themselves 'atheists' or 'agnostics'; terminology and labels are unimportant. The fact is,

---

* See Dave Tomlinson, *How to Be a Bad Christian – and a better human being* (Hodder & Stoughton, 2012).

hordes of people recognise that life is more than its externals, more than a purely material existence, and they look for something more consequential. However, traditional religious explanations of this no longer ring true – not least because they are encased in theological dogma that has largely lost its force and credibility. A religion based on required beliefs is no longer viable.

Possibly the greatest drawback with the now burgeoning religionless spirituality is that it tends to be individualistic. When the Church and organised religion become sidelined, no alternative spiritual community exists to take their place. Sanderson Jones and Pippa Evans recognised this when in 2013 they launched the Sunday Assembly, a secular version of church with the motto 'live better, help often, wonder more'. Life is short, their website states, 'it is brilliant, it is sometimes tough – we build communities that help everyone live life as fully as possible'.

I am a great supporter of the Sunday Assembly, and of any endeavour to create spiritually enriching community. But I am also a Christian, a passionate follower of Jesus, and I believe that Christianity can still offer something vital and dynamic to the world of the twenty-first century, *provided we will allow ourselves to be transformed in the process*. If the Church in effect says, 'This is who we are;

this is what we have to say – take it or leave it,' then most people will leave it, and the Church and Christianity will become, as Bonhoeffer predicted, a religious enclave at the edges of life instead of a powerful force for spiritual renewal at the centre.

I believe we need a resurgence of Christian liberality: a generous-minded, big-hearted faith that will create a welcoming spiritual home for today's postmodern pilgrims, those black sheep and prodigals who have wandered from the fold, and many others who never went near the fold in the first place yet hanker after space for a soul to belong.

Such faith will not focus on creeds and doctrines, but on *a way to be* in the world. It will be about compassion, justice and peace, about spiritual evolution, community and transformation, not dogma. In a 'world come of age', religion based on subscribing to mandatory beliefs is no longer viable apart from in the religious ghetto. As Gandhi and others have pointed out, Jesus is Christianity's best asset: not beliefs about him but Jesus the human being, who showed what divinity looks like in flesh and blood reality, and called us to imitate him, to be part of his way.

After reading one of my books, someone recently emailed and wrote, 'I see you as a devotee of Christ, not as a Christian.' And yes, I am far more interested in Jesus

231

than Christianity. I have a long history with the Christian community, I am a loyal priest within the Christian Church and I am fascinated by Christian theology, but my fundamental passion is learning to follow the way of Jesus. I don't know what the future holds for Christianity, but I am utterly convinced that Jesus Christ and the message of the kingdom of God that he embodied will continue to grip the hearts and minds of people as long as the world stands.

In a 'world come of age' people are less trusting of authority figures, but they need a model of humanity to inspire and draw them into a greater state of spiritual evolution. For me, that model is Jesus. As Richard Rohr states, 'This is how Jesus "causes" our salvation. It is not a magic act accomplished by moral behaviour; rather, salvation is a gradual *realisation* of who we are – and always have been – and will be eternally.'*

Part of the saving process Jesus initiated was to create a 'companionship of empowerment': a community of hope and inclusion that enabled people to see themselves as whole human beings; to start to become all that they could be. He not only gathered a rag-tag bunch of misfits as the core of his beloved community, he wined and dined

---

* Richard Rohr, *Eager to Love: The Alternative Way of Francis of Assisi* (Hodder & Stoughton, 2014).

with those whom the religious la-di-da labelled 'sinners': prostitutes, publicans, tax collectors, people shoved into the margins of society – these were his friends.

There are two circular tables in my life. The first is in our dining room, a beautiful piece of pine furniture created by a woman carpenter in Yorkshire. I love nothing more than hosting a bunch of people around this table, eating and drinking, swapping ideas, telling stories that make us laugh or cry. It's a table without a head, where everyone has a place. I especially love it when we have too many people gathered, so it becomes a bit of a squash, where bodies, food, drink and conversations almost merge.

The other table is our round altar in St Luke's, where Christ hosts a larger gathering of people, black and white, male and female, gay and straight, Christians, doubters and atheists. One Holocaust Memorial Day, a company of Jewish friends surrounded the table with us; Muslims and Buddhists have been there, some pagans too. But it doesn't end there: each of us brings a whole tribe of loved ones to the table – absent in body yet present in spirit. And as we take bread and wine 'which earth has given and human hands have made', we also recognise that all creation is crammed into this space: our round table becomes an *axis mundi*, a world centre or celestial pole.

For me, the image of a round table brilliantly symbolises the sort of Church required as we move forward in the twenty-first century: a place of generosity, companionship, inclusion, equality and dialogue.

Dietrich Bonhoeffer said that the Church is the Church only when it exists for others, i.e. when it ceases to be a hemmed-in sheepfold and becomes an enormous welcoming space, where people can breathe and grow and evolve – and maybe share a few Hobnobs!

15. I believe in straying from the beaten track

not all those who wander are lost

*I may not have gone where I intended to go, but I
think I have ended up where I needed to be.*
Douglas Adams, *The Long Dark Tea Time
of the Soul*

It surprised some people when I invited an evangelical friend,
a biblical scholar, to lead an evening at Holy Joes. In fact, *he*
was probably the most surprised of all. But I feel it cannot
possibly be a good thing to listen only to those you agree with.

Being considerably more conservative, theologically, than the rest of us, I wondered what my friend would make of our quirky gathering, and how Holy Joes would cope with him.

We had a full house: fifty or sixty people crammed into the upstairs room of the Alexandra pub on Clapham Common. To help our visitor acclimatise, I invited people to say in a few words how they came to be part of Holy Joes and what it meant to them.

In response (with a twinkle in his eye), he said, 'I notice that many of you speak of being on a spiritual journey – which is great. But I would like to ask: is it a journey or a wander?' It was a good question, which prompted almost ninety minutes of animated discussion. He relished every single one of them. At the close, he said, 'It's been great fun. I love your banter, your directness and your energy. But I am still left wondering where it all leads, where you will land up. And whether that matters to you.'

Journey or wander, Holy Joes did not exist to convert people or get them back on track. That was the kind of approach they came to Holy Joes to escape. What they wanted was adult discussion about faith issues: to be free to argue and disagree with impunity, to be irreverent at times (we were good at that!), and to go through an evening without someone trying to put them right. Our discussions were raucous, difficult to keep on track, often passionate, sometimes moving – and faith-saving, many would say. At least six regulars went on to be ordained.

Personally, I like a good wander. It's how I approach life in general. My holiday nightmare would be to go on one of those package deals, complete with a daily schedule, a tour guide and obligatory outings. It might suit some people, but it would be living hell for me. I like to make it up as I go along, to have the freedom to mosey around and explore. If a small town appears, or a lake, or a backroad, I want to wander off, stop around for a day or two, be surprised, turn up something new and unexpected.

My attitude to faith is similar: I am attracted to theological sidetracks. I like to deviate from the straight and narrow, to burrow and explore. If something is declared off-limits, I am immediately impelled to take a closer look. Earlier in the book, I mentioned that the term heresy originally referred to the 'act of choosing'; to be a heretic simply meant to 'choose for oneself'. But over time heresy came to denote a belief or an opinion considered erroneous – at odds with the official position. Then, heretics started to be excluded, excommunicated, and worse.

And why? Surely it is a good thing for people to think for themselves, to have different opinions, even if most of us disagree with them. Surely it is a sign of a mature, healthy community when it can accommodate dissent, when people will fight for the right of others to hold a different view. And who knows: maybe, in the end, they will turn out to be right, and we will be glad they were there.

Some people approach Christian tradition as if it were an exclusive club where certain ideas, doctrines and practices are conserved, treated as sacrosanct. If someone deviates from them – for example, by questioning the Bible in some way, or by supporting the ordination of women or legitimising same-sex marriage – they are decried for abandoning traditional Christianity.

Yet, in reality, Christian tradition works like a vast, unending conversation – sometimes an all-out row – that changes and evolves from one generation to the next. Continuity with the past is maintained, but also an engagement with the present, so that new insights from science, psychology and wider social understanding help to influence and shape the discussion. At its healthiest, far from excluding those who deviate from the beaten track, tradition incorporates diverse contributions within an ever-evolving, vigorous debate. Deviant opinions and wandering ideas simply stimulate the conversation, adding spice and creativity.

Parallel to this, social scientists talk about two kinds of organisation. The first, a *closed flow system*, tends to resist change; its exponents cling to predictability and perpetuate existing ideas and patterns of behaviour. It requires conformity, creates a defence against new influences and opposes departure from the established path.

But there are also *open flow systems* of organisation, where new ideas and fresh influences are welcomed to become part of an ever-transforming framework. Here, the assumption is that newcomers will bring fresh impetus and innovation that will enrich and enhance overall effectiveness.

The importance of such creative openness in a group or organisation is witnessed in the talking circles of the Blackfoot people in North America. These are the organisational centre of the Blackfoot community, the forum where decisions are made. But they are always careful to leave a gap for the new to enter, a physical gap that represents an openness to new ideas and influences that may prove vital to future growth.

Rigid organisations and traditions mostly see those who stray from the path as troublemakers, irritants or detractors. Yet people who are never satisfied to let well enough alone often turn out to be the creative thinkers that the organisation or tradition needs in order to move forward. *Even the most beaten of tracks was once a wilderness.*

The most famous wanderer in the Bible is the prodigal son – not the best exemplar for legitimate meandering, you may think. Yet it is well worth taking a second look. The story is well known, but let me offer my quick-fire unauthorised version:

Dad has two sons. Younger son asks Dad for his inheritance early. Dad gives it to him, son squanders it, becomes homeless. Then, out of desperation, son decides to go home and see if he can work for his dad as a hired hand. Meanwhile, older son is working himself silly at home, doing what Dad wants. Dad spots the wandering son returning home and runs to meet him. Gives him hugs and kisses and welcomes him back. Then Dad tells the servants to go and kill the fatted calf so that they can invite all their friends and celebrate. Older son is seriously fed up about Dad's insane extravagance toward his ne'er-do-well brother, complaining that in all the years he's worked faithfully on the farm, his dad hasn't ever given him a party. Dad reassures older son that everything now belongs to him, but that his brother who was *lost is now found, and that's a very good reason to party.**

I sometimes read out the story to an audience before inviting them to spend a few minutes meditating upon it. The narrative has three characters. I ask people to let their minds move freely between them, and notice which one they are drawn towards. I then request the audience to put words into the mouth of that particular character – not the words in the text, but their own imagined words – and then speak them out. After initial reluctance, the audience mostly co-operates, and increasingly gains confidence to be more imaginative and candid in what they get the characters to say. Later, I invite everyone to reflect on what the exercise might reveal about their own thoughts, motives or feelings on the issues raised.

Fascinatingly, I find that most people (around 75 per cent of any given audience) choose to put words into the mouth of the older brother, saying, with increasing passion and feeling, things like:

'It's not fair! I've always tried to be a good person.'

'Why should he have all the fun?'

'My dad must be stupid!'

---

* My version of Luke 15:11–32.

'Wait until I get my brother on his own!'

'I wish I had a bit of riotous living.'

'I wonder what lies out there.'

'Why am I so boring?'

'Why am I so angry? I could have gone too. Maybe I will go.'

It's almost as if people are speaking out of their own feelings and experiences which, of course, is the point.

I have no doubt that the general tendency to focus on the older brother is entirely in line with what Jesus intended. The parable of the prodigal son is one of three stories (along with the lost sheep and the lost coin) that Jesus told in response to the Pharisees and scribes grumbling when they saw him hanging out with 'sinners', and eating and drinking with them. I don't think the object of the story is to say what a wretched sinner the prodigal is, but to highlight the scandalous grace of the father; also, the awful sadness that some people may choose to live their entire lives in self-righteous misery.

I find it reassuring that Jesus appeared to enjoy the company of sinners more than that of pious scribes and Pharisees. I, too, often feel most at home with people whose lives are messy or chaotic. Some of my most enjoyable experiences as a priest (also my most effective) are in the pub after a funeral or a wedding, or at a party: resisting lovely, generous people trying to get me drunk, dancing to George Michael, Abba or Britney, listening to *ad hoc* confessions above the hubbub, speaking words of forgiveness, and sometimes even saying prayers with people over a pint of beer in a quiet corner of the room.

For me, church doesn't get any better than this!

The overwhelming majority of sermons, poems and writings on the parable of the prodigal naturally focus on the son's return. One of my own favourites is Henri Nouwen's little book *The Return of the Prodigal Son: A Story of Homecoming*, which offers a moving and personal meditation on Rembrandt's painting of the event.

However, I also love Rainer Maria Rilke's poem, 'The Departure of the Prodigal Son', which takes a different tack. Perhaps, influenced by his own experience of being ejected from his father's home against his will, Rilke looks at the story in a quite different light, concentrating on the son's departure instead of his return. Maybe the prodigal's journey into the unknown is not selfish, Rilke seems to suggest, but brave: an adventure in which he not only tastes a newfound freedom but finds God.

Holy Joes certainly functioned as a magnet for church prodigals: those who felt hemmed in, frustrated and even abused in their experience of churches. One darling young man who had been thrown out of his church after being courageous enough to reveal his sexual orientation unsurprisingly turned his back on Christianity and God. He then embarked on a near-deliberate quest to contract HIV, which he did, before coming home to himself and to a community that loved and embraced him for who he was (he survived HIV and is doing fine).

The question as to why prodigals depart is far more complex than sometimes presumed. Luke's gospel doesn't elaborate on the point, but I definitely believe it is a mistake to imagine that those who set out on hedonistic or self-destructive lifestyles, or who run away from home or church, or who drop out of their responsibilities are necessarily bad people, or even people making deliberately bad choices; the reality is often greatly more complicated than that.

However, the really big question that intrigues me when I read the parable is: What happened next? The story in Luke's gospel is open-ended, unfinished. Luke seems to want us to imagine the rest. Personally, I strongly hope that the older brother chilled out, joined in the party; maybe went on some adventures of his own. But what of the prodigal? What happened next for him? In the margin of his Bible, next to the parable, the theologian Paul

Tillich wrote, 'When the prodigal son came home, I hope he didn't stay long.' I literally punched the air when I stumbled on this quote; it's what I have been saying in sermons for years.

Most of all, I hope the younger brother didn't turn into his older sibling. I hope he didn't become dreary and dutiful, still less self-righteous about his return. I hope he didn't 'grow up' and lose his impishness. I hope he continued wandering – finding better journeys to go on, but wandering still. Any inclination to use the story as an inducement to toe the line, or conform to religious or social expectations makes me cringe.

Maybe we need a different notion of prodigality. Let's face it: for most of us, the word 'prodigal' is hardly part of our daily vocabulary. Its meaning, which is now deeply coloured by the parable, has become synonymous with being wayward or disobedient, a loser. Yet 'prodigal' literally means 'wastefully extravagant'. And while that may indeed suggest being wanton, promiscuous or profligate, it can surely be interpreted in a different way.

For example, wasn't the father wastefully extravagant in his treatment of his younger son? Wasn't his behaviour prodigal too? Not too many family counsellors would commend his liberality in granting his son's wish to have his inheritance prematurely. Surely, he knew what his son was like. Wasn't it predictable that the immature boy would blow the lot? Yet the father is universally taken as a representation of God.

Then later, when his son returns, the father splashes out on him with preposterous, prodigal extravagance. He never even waited to hear his son's rehearsed apology before falling all over him with hugs and kisses, giving him the feast to end all feasts. Little wonder the diligent older brother was disgusted.

The big mistake is to imagine that the parable contrasts responsibility with prodigality. That isn't what this story is about. Instead, it contrasts two kinds of prodigality, two kinds of squandering: that of the son's self-destructive extravagance, and the wastefully extravagant love of his father.

Apart from proclaiming the reckless generosity of divine grace, this parable tells me that God is not pointlessly prudish about the things people get up to; what God primarily cares about is what people do to themselves and others in the process. The father in the story has no checklist of naughty things his son did. He doesn't take the boy through each one, squeezing out detailed confessions. The text simply says that the son 'came to himself', then returned home. And that, apparently, was enough.

THE JOURNEY
David Whyte

Above the mountains
the geese turn into
the light again

painting their
black silhouettes
on an open sky.

Sometimes everything
has to be
inscribed across
the heavens

so you can find
the one line
already written
inside you.

Sometimes it takes
a great sky
to find that

first, bright
and indescribable
wedge of freedom
in your own heart.

Sometimes with
the bones of the black
sticks left when the fire
has gone out

someone has written
something new
in the ashes
of your life.

You are not leaving.
Even as the light
fades quickly now,
*you are arriving.**

David Whyte wrote 'The Journey' for a friend who had
gone through the agony of departing from a long-standing

---

* David Whyte, 'The Journey', *River Flow: New & Selected Poems
1984–2007*, (Many Rivers Press, Langley Washington, 2007). Used by
permission.

marriage. As she went through the process of being stripped of the hopes and dreams she had shared with her husband for their relationship, Whyte says he witnessed a very powerful, very simple new internal identity starting to make itself known in her.

We all need to go on our own existential quest, which is always a search for God, whether we realise it or not, but also a search for our own true self. Thankfully, this need not involve the breakup of a relationship, or the sort of chaos and turmoil that the prodigal experienced; we don't all have to go on life-shattering benders or suffer the pain of a divorce. But there are always things to leave behind, to depart from, not least the beaten track of other people's opinions and expectations – the crippling expectations we lay upon ourselves.

Then, finally, we will be able to greet our own self, arriving at our own door, and, smiling, stand tall on the inside to declare: 'This is me! This is who I am! I have arrived. I am home.'

Postscript: Liberal evangelism

why I still think Jesus is the answer
(depending on the question)

My book *How to Be a Bad Christian – and a Better Human Being* was launched in the beer tent at Greenbelt Festival in 2012. The publisher cut a deal with the brewery to rename one of the beers 'Bad Christian', which proved very popular – the beer, that is. People still ask me where they can buy it!

The weather on the day of the launch was foul – perfect festival conditions. We waded through inches of mud to reach the bustling canvas pub – 'The Jesus Arms'. Even the tent floor was covered in sludge. But no one cared.

After a rabble-rousing evening (free beers on the publisher definitely helped), a friend commented, 'You were on fire tonight, Dave.'

'Like a liberal evangelist,' someone else quipped.

I laughed, but later lay awake in bed with the phrase going through my mind: *liberal evangelist*. It sounded like an oxymoron. The liberal and evangelical approaches to faith often represent different ends of the spectrum. But in the wee small hours, the combination appealed to me.

I believe the world needs a generous-spirited, progressively minded faith – *proclaimed with all the zeal and passion of an evangelist*. Black and white religion, like black and white thinking in general, is a large part of the problem with the world, and definitely not the way forward.

Black and white religion generates an 'us and them' mentality. It interprets sacred texts and traditions in a way that locks us into the past instead of thrusting us into the future. It feeds our fear of difference instead of helping us to see beyond it. It imposes prescribed beliefs and morals that inhibit us from thinking for ourselves and discovering what we really believe deep down. Basically, black and white religion stunts the growth of spiritual intelligence.

I recall a cartoon with someone holding a sign that said 'Christ is the answer'. And behind was another person with a sign saying 'What was the question?' I don't believe that the sectarian Christ of black and white Christianity is the answer to anything. But the Jesus I find in the Gospels helps to answer a lot of things: the Jesus who championed the poor and the marginalised, who treated women as real people at a time when they were the chattels of a patriarchal society, the Jesus who forgave his killers and invited a dying thief to join him in paradise.

If this Jesus were here today, I believe he would lead his disciples on a Pride march, he would be in refugee camps helping people to find a life apart from guns and bombs, he would support the sexually abused and also liberate their offenders from the self-hatred that drives them to harm others. I believe the Jesus of the Gospels would still be weeping over Jerusalem and supporting those who strive for justice and reconciliation in the Middle East. I believe he would call vigorously for the pulling down of all walls, literal and metaphorical.

I am a Christian, but I have little interest in spreading Christianity. I am far more interested in fuelling a new Jesus movement. As Karen Armstrong writes, 'Jesus did not spend a great deal of time discoursing about the trinity or original sin or the incarnation, which have preoccupied later Christians. He went around doing good and being compassionate.'*

But in the end, there is not much good in just thinking about what Jesus might do if he were here today. What is important – vital, actually – is to discover the spirit of Jesus in our own hearts, and to get out there and let that shine through.

Live passionately! Believe sceptically! Love extravagantly!

* In Steve Paulson, *Atoms & Eden: Conversations on Religion & Science* (Oxford University Press, 2010).

Acknowledgements

I have dedicated this book to Peter Thomson, one of the most charming and lovable black sheep I have ever known. An Australian Anglican priest, noted for his influence on the young Tony Blair, Peter was a committed Christian socialist and an outstandingly irreverent reverend.

When the Bishop of Melbourne fired Peter early in his ministry, he left the ecclesiastical courtroom in disgust and peed on the lawn. The 'offence' that lost him his job was to take work as a teacher in order to raise funds for his poor parish. He further alarmed the authorities when he proposed to raise more money by having his wife open a hairdressing salon inside his church.

Peter died in January 2010. His influence is felt throughout this book. It was Peter who introduced me to the world-renowned Catholic theologian Hans Küng, who I write about in chapter 13. Peter had arranged for Küng to have dinner with Tony Blair, but floods in the North of England called the Prime Minister away. Peter suggested that, instead, we invite Küng to the vicarage. It was a scary moment when I collected one of the greatest

Christian thinkers of our time from 10 Downing Street and brought him to our table.

I am very grateful to Peter for showing me what being a black sheep means: pursuing one's passion regardless of the consequences.

I am also deeply thankful to my beloved Pat who sacrificed so much of our time together to let me complete this project, and who effectively kept the world at bay when I needed solitude. Her grounded wisdom and common sense guide my thinking and keep my feet on the ground, always.

I often say that everyone needs an editor (whether they write or not!), and I am indebted to my friend Katherine Venn whose editorial guidance sometimes saved me from myself and made this book much better than it would otherwise have been. And a huge thank you to all the Hodder Faith team for believing in me and bringing this venture to birth.

Thank you to my gorgeous pal, Rob Pepper, artist extraordinaire, whose amazing pictures transform this book from just another pile of words into an object of beauty. Thank you also to my friend and colleague Martin Wroe, whose spirited fun and imagination energise my thinking; and to the flock of black sheep at St Luke's, a church I am proud to be a part of, as well as all the people who allow me to tell their stories.

Do you wish this wasn't the end?
Are you hungry for more great teaching, inspiring
testimonies, ideas to challenge your faith?

Join us at www.hodderfaith.com, follow us on Twitter
or find us on Facebook to make sure you get the latest from
your favourite authors.

Including interviews, videos, articles, competitions
and opportunities to tell us just what you thought about
our latest releases.